MathFlare

Name: _______________________

Class: __________

Teacher: _______________________

Introduction

As parents and educators, we recognize the pivotal role mathematics plays in shaping a child's academic journey and future success. Yet, the path to mathematical proficiency can often seem daunting, fraught with challenges and complexities. That's where the transformative power of MathFlare Workbooks shine through, illuminating the way forward with clarity, precision, and purpose.

Introducing MathFlare Workbooks – a beacon of guidance, a testament to excellence, and a catalyst for achievement. Crafted with meticulous care and expertise, MathFlare Workbooks stand as paragons of educational excellence, designed to nurture young minds, ignite a passion for learning, and develop a deep-rooted understanding of mathematical concepts.

Picture this: your child eagerly delves into the pages of Mathflare Workbook, greeted by a step-by-step guide illuminated with vivid examples that demystify complex mathematical concepts. With each turn of the page, they embark on a journey of discovery, encountering thoughtfully curated practice questions that reinforce learning and hone problem-solving skills. And when they unveil the answers to those very questions, a sense of accomplishment blossoms within them – a tangible reward for their hard work and dedication.

But MathFlare Workbooks are more than just tools for learning; they are pathways to comprehension, fostering a deep-seated understanding of mathematical concepts through a sequential, logical flow. From fundamental principles to advanced problem-solving strategies, every chapter builds upon the last, ensuring a robust foundation upon which future knowledge can be constructed.

As parents, we yearn for nothing more than to see our children thrive, to witness the spark of inspiration ignited within them as they conquer academic challenges with confidence and poise. MathFlare Workbooks serve as partners in this noble endeavor, offering not just practice questions, but the keys to unlocking a world of opportunity.

And for teachers, MathFlare Workbooks stand as invaluable allies in the quest to cultivate mathematical proficiency in the classroom. With answers readily available, instructors can focus on guiding and nurturing their students, confident in the knowledge that MathFlare Workbooks provide a solid framework upon which to build.

In the pages of MathFlare Workbooks, we find not just the promise of academic excellence, but the seeds of a brighter tomorrow. So let us embrace the power of mathematics, let us champion the journey of learning, and let us pave the way for a generation of young minds poised to shape the world. With MathFlare Workbooks as our guide, the possibilities are infinite, and the future, bright.

Table of Contents

Integers, Ratio and Percent	
Positive and Negative Integers	1
Proportional Relationship	11
Percents	19
Convert Percent and Decimals	34
Percent Word Problems	39
Convert Ratios, Fractions, Percents, Decimals	50

MathFlare
MATH WORKBOOK
Grade 2
Step by Step Guide and Essential Practice with Answers
Addition Subtraction
Multiplication
Place Value and Expanded Notations
Geometry
MathFlare Publishing

MathFlare
MATH WORKBOOK
Grade 2-3
Step by Step Guide and Essential Practice with Answers
Addition Subtraction
Multiplication and Division
Place Value and Expanded Notations
Geometry
MathFlare Publishing

MathFlare
MATH WORKBOOK
Grade 3
Step by Step Guide and Essential Practice with Answers
Multiplication and Division
Decimals
Place Value and Expanded Notations
Fractions and Geometry
MathFlare Publishing

MathFlare
MATH WORKBOOK
Grade 1
Step by Step Guide and Essential Practice with Answers
Counting and Numbers
Addition and Subtraction
Place Value and Expanded Notations
Understanding Time
MathFlare Publishing

MathFlare
MATH WORKBOOK
Grade 1-2
Step by Step Guide and Essential Practice with Answers
Counting and Numbers
Addition and Subtraction
Place Value and Expanded Notations
Understanding Time
MathFlare Publishing

MathFlare
MATH WORKBOOK
Grade 3-4
Step by Step Guide and Essential Practice with Answers
Addition Subtraction
Multiplication Division
Place Value and Expanded Notations
Fractions and Geometry
MathFlare Publishing

MathFlare
MATH WORKBOOK
Grade 4
Step by Step Guide and Essential Practice with Answers
Addition Subtraction
Multiplication Division
Place Value and Expanded Notations
Fractions and Geometry
MathFlare Publishing

MathFlare
MATH WORKBOOK
Grade 4-5
Step by Step Guide and Essential Practice with Answers
Multiplication Division
Place Value and Expanded Notations
Fractions and Geometry
Unit Conversion
MathFlare Publishing

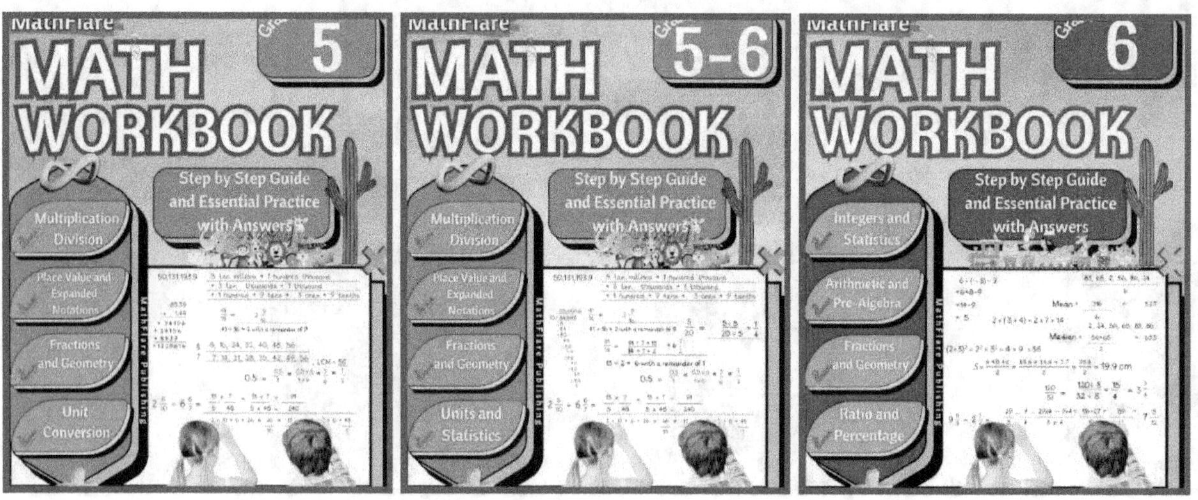

MathFlare
MATH WORKBOOK
5
Step by Step Guide and Essential Practice with Answers
Multiplication Division
Place Value and Expanded Notations
Fractions and Geometry
Unit Conversion
MathFlare Publishing

MathFlare
MATH WORKBOOK
5-6
Step by Step Guide and Essential Practice with Answers
Multiplication Division
Place Value and Expanded Notations
Fractions and Geometry
Units and Statistics
MathFlare Publishing

MathFlare
MATH WORKBOOK
6
Step by Step Guide and Essential Practice with Answers
Integers and Statistics
Arithmetic and Pre-Algebra
Fractions and Geometry
Ratio and Percentage
MathFlare Publishing

MathFlare
MATH WORKBOOK
6-7
Step by Step Guide and Essential Practice with Answers
Arithmetic and Pre-Algebra
Ratio, Percent Proportion
Geometry
Statistics
MathFlare Publishing

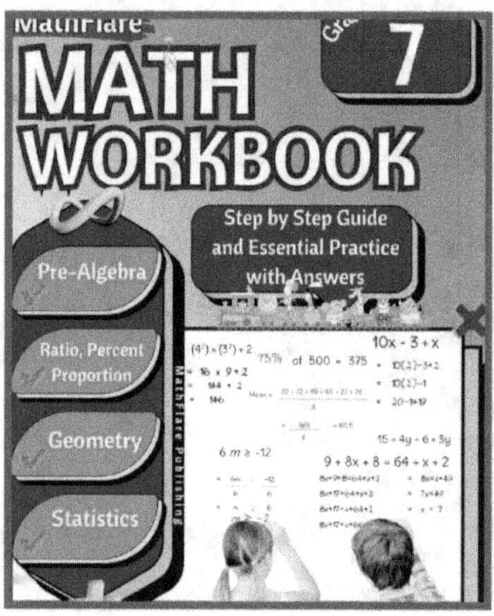

MathFlare
MATH WORKBOOK
7
Step by Step Guide and Essential Practice with Answers
Pre-Algebra
Ratio, Percent Proportion
Geometry
Statistics
MathFlare Publishing

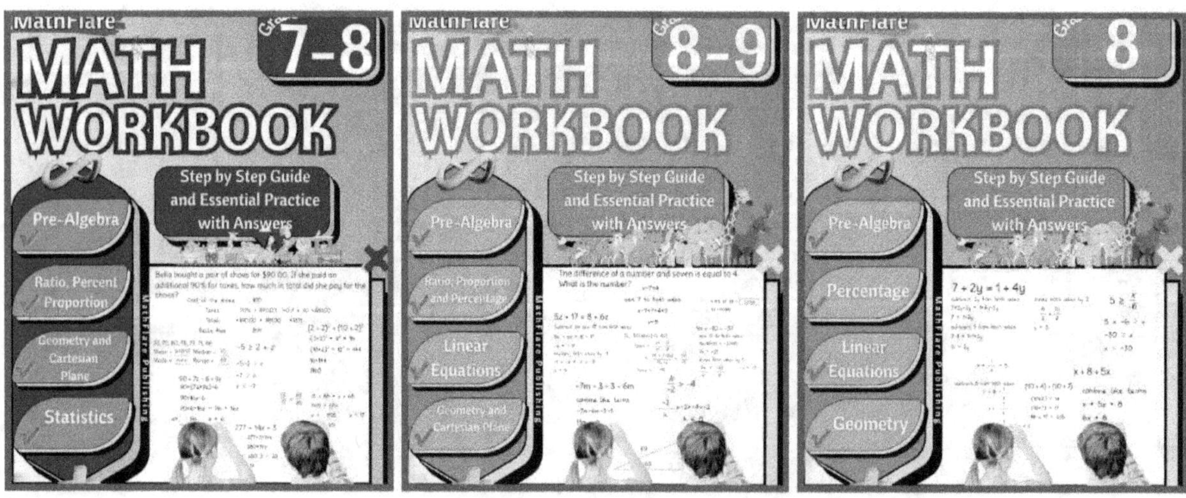

MathFlare
MATH WORKBOOK
7-8
Step by Step Guide and Essential Practice with Answers
Pre-Algebra
Ratio, Percent Proportion
Geometry and Cartesian Plane
Statistics
MathFlare Publishing

MathFlare
MATH WORKBOOK
8-9
Step by Step Guide and Essential Practice with Answers
Pre-Algebra
Ratio, Proportion and Percentage
Linear Equations
Geometry and Cartesian Plane
MathFlare Publishing

MathFlare
MATH WORKBOOK
8
Step by Step Guide and Essential Practice with Answers
Pre-Algebra
Percentage
Linear Equations
Geometry
MathFlare Publishing

Positive and Negrative Integers

Positive and negative integers are whole numbers that can represent quantities greater than zero and less than zero, respectively.

Positive Integers: Positive integers are whole numbers greater than zero. They are denoted by the numbers 1,2,3,4...

Negative Integers: Negative integers are whole numbers less than zero. They are denoted by placing a negative sign ("-") before the numbers, such as $-1, -2, -3, -4, ...$

The positive integers are used to represent the number of objects, scores, etc. whereas the negative integers can be used to represent debt, losses, temperatures below freezing points, etc.

Let's solve some problems:

1. $6 - (-8) - 9$

- Start by simplifying within the parentheses:

$$-(-8) \text{ becomes } 8.$$

- Rewrite the expression with the simplified part:

$$6 + 8 - 9.$$

- Now perform addition and subtraction from left to right:

$$6 + 8 = 14, \text{ then } 14 - 9 = 5$$

2. $(-5) - (-3) + 10$

$$(-5) + 3 + 10$$

$$(-5) + 3 = -2, \text{ then } -2 + 10 = 8$$

Ratio and Proportion and Percentage

A proportional relationship between two quantities exists when they have a constant ratio or when one is a multiple of the other. In other words, if we increase one quantity, the other quantity will increase or decrease by the same factor. For example, if we double one quantity, the other quantity will also double.

Let's solve a problem:

$$\frac{}{9} = \frac{8}{18}$$

Step 1: Cross Multiply: Cross multiply by multiplying the numerator of one fraction by the denominator of the other, and vice versa:

$$x \times 18 = 9 \times 8$$

Step 2: Solve for the Unknown: Perform the multiplication on both sides of the equation:

$$18x = 72$$

Step 3: Divide Both Sides by the Coefficient of the Unknown: To isolate x, divide both sides of the equation by the coefficient of x, which is 18:

$$\frac{18x}{18} = \frac{72}{18}$$

$$x = 4$$

Step 4: Verify Check your solution by substituting x = 4 back into the original equation:

$$\frac{4}{9} = \frac{8}{18}$$

Since both sides are equal, the solution x = 4 is correct.

Ratio and Proportion Word Problems

We can use the concept of proportionality in solving many word problems, for example:

If a car travels 620 miles in six hours, how far can it travel in 12 hours?

Since the car travels a certain distance in a certain amount of time, we can assume that the distance traveled is directly proportional to the time taken.

Let d be the distance the car can travel in 12 hours.

We can set up a proportion:

$$\frac{\text{Distance1}}{\text{Time1}} = \frac{\text{Distance2}}{\text{Time2}}$$

Substituting the given values:

$$\frac{620 \text{ miles}}{6 \text{ hours}} = \frac{d}{12 \text{ hours}}$$

Now, let's solve for d.

$$d = \frac{620 \times 12}{6} = \frac{7440}{6} = 1240$$

So, the car can travel 1240 miles in 12 hours.

Percentage

Percentage is a way of expressing a number as a fraction of 100. It is commonly used to represent proportions, rates, and comparisons. The symbol "%" is used to denote percentages.

To calculate a percentage, we multiply the given number by the appropriate fraction or decimal equivalent.

How to calculate a percentage:

Convert Percentage to Decimal: If the percentage is given as a percentage value (e.g., 25%), convert it to its decimal equivalent by dividing by 100.

$$\text{For example, 25\% as a decimal is } \frac{25}{100} = 0.25$$

Multiply: Multiply the decimal equivalent of the percentage by the given number. This gives us the portion of the number that represents the percentage.

$$100 \times 0.25 = 25\%$$

Result: The result is the calculated percentage value.

For example, to calculate 25% of 80:

<u>Convert 25% to a decimal</u>: 25% = 0.25.

<u>Multiply 0.25 by 80</u>: 0.25 × 80 = 20. The result is 20.

Percent Word Problems

Percent word problems involve situations where percentages are used to calculate quantities or amounts. These problems often require converting percentages to decimals and then applying them to the given values.

For example:

Bella bought a pair of shoes for $90.00. If she paid an additional 90% for taxes, how much in total did she pay for the shoes?

- Bella bought a pair of shoes for $90.00.

- She paid an additional 90% for taxes.

Calculate 90% of $90:

$$Tax = 90\% \times 90$$

$$Tax = 0.90 \times 90$$

$$Tax = \$81$$

Add the tax amount to the original price:

$$Total\ cost = \$90 + \$81$$

$$Total\ cost = \$171$$

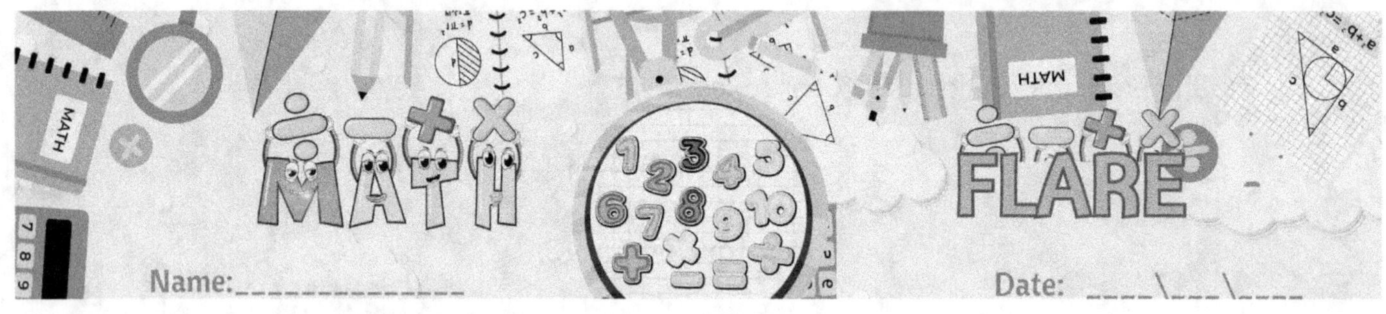

Positive and Negative Integers
Evaluate.

1. $3 - (6 + 10) + 1 =$

2. $2 - (1 + 7) - 6 =$

3. $(-3) + (-10) - 7 =$

4. $7 + 8 - 10 =$

5. $10 - (4 + 2) + 8 =$

6. $(-10) + (-3) + 7 =$

7. $9 - (5 - 5) =$

8. $(10 - 2) - (7 - 8) =$

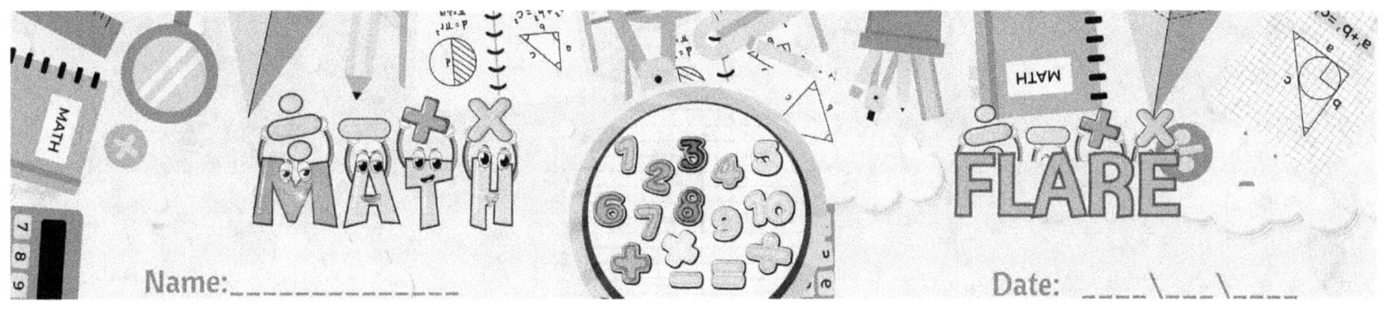

9. $7 - (3 + 8) + 7 =$

10. $(-7) - (-2) =$

11. $9 - (9 - 2) =$

12. $8 + (-3) - 6 =$

13. $6 - 4 - 6 - 8 =$

14. $7 - 6 - (4 + 2) =$

15. $7 - (6 + 3) - 6 =$

16. $(-3) - (-1) + 1 =$

17. $5 - (1 + 5) - 1 =$

18. $10 + 4 - 10 =$

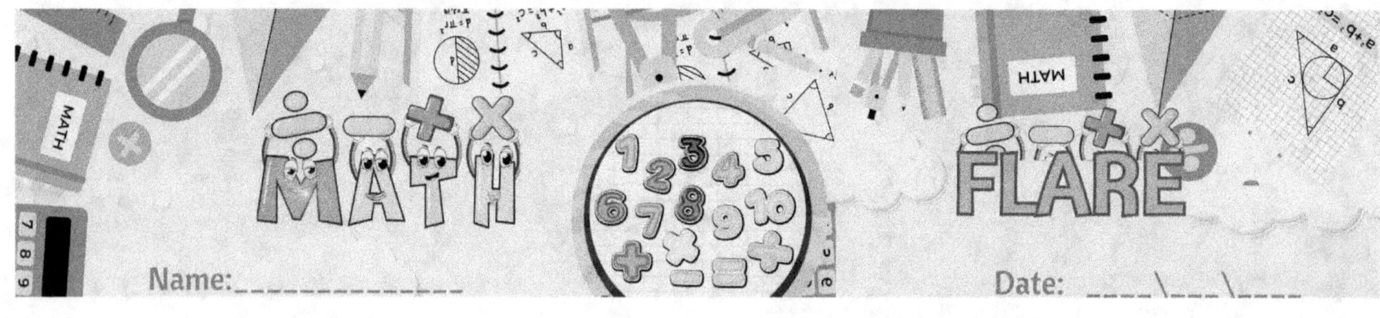

19. $(9 + 1) + (2 - 1) =$

20. $10 - (7 + 2) - 1 =$

21. $3 + 4 - (5 + 5) =$

22. $(-7) + 3 + (-3) =$

23. $7 - (-9) =$

24. $4 - (9 + 6) - 1 =$

25. $1 - 10 + 2 =$

26. $5 - (6 - 2) =$

27. $4 - 8 - (8 + 8) =$

28. $(3 - 2) + (7 + 6) =$

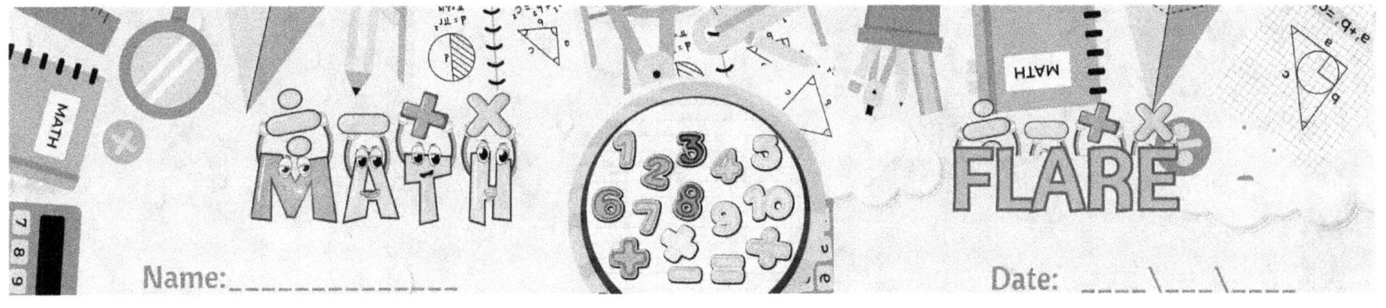

Name:_________________________

Date: _____________

29. $(-5) + 6 + (-7) =$

30. $(-6) + 8 + (-1) =$

31. $(6 - 4) - (10 + 1) =$

32. $(9 - 4) - 8 =$

33. $2 - (5 + 7) - 8 =$

34. $1 + (-9) - 9 =$

35. $9 - 2 - 1 - 7 =$

36. $5 - 5 + (-9) =$

37. $3 - 6 + 7 =$

38. $2 + (3 - 1) =$

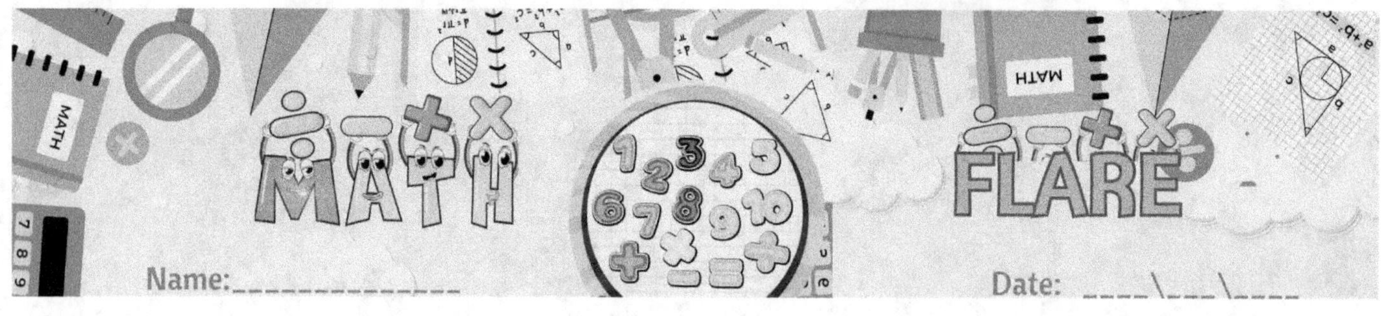

39. $8 + (9 - 2) =$

40. $(2 - 8) + (2 + 6) =$

41. $6 + (-8) =$

42. $10 + (-1) =$

43. $6 - 2 + 4 =$

44. $2 - 4 - 1 - 10 =$

45. $2 - (4 - 8) =$

46. $7 + (-4) + 6 =$

47. $1 - 2 + (-3) =$

48. $(3 - 3) + 9 - 3 =$

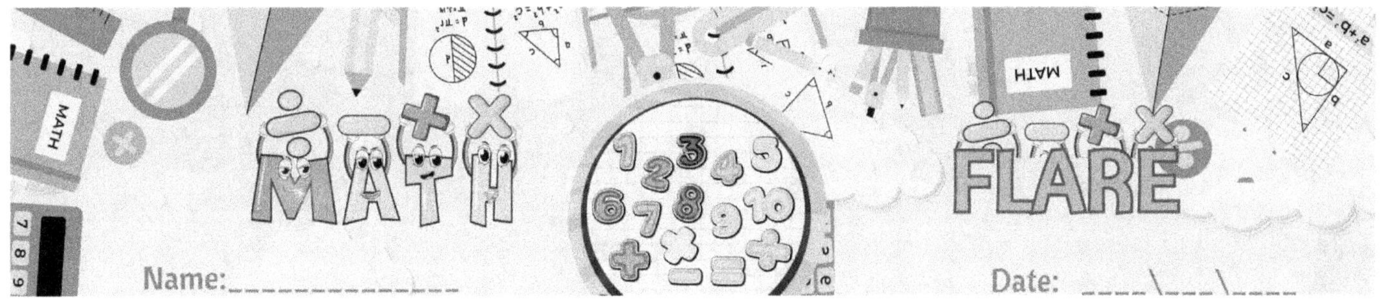

49. $9 - 7 - 4 - 1 =$

50. $4 - (3 - 5) =$

51. $(-10) + (-10) + 4 =$

52. $3 - 1 - (2 + 10) =$

53. $1 - (-4) =$

54. $2 - 7 - (10 + 5) =$

55. $(7 + 1) - (9 - 3) =$

56. $(1 - 5) - (7 - 2) =$

57. $7 + 10 - 4 =$

58. $4 + (9 - 7) =$

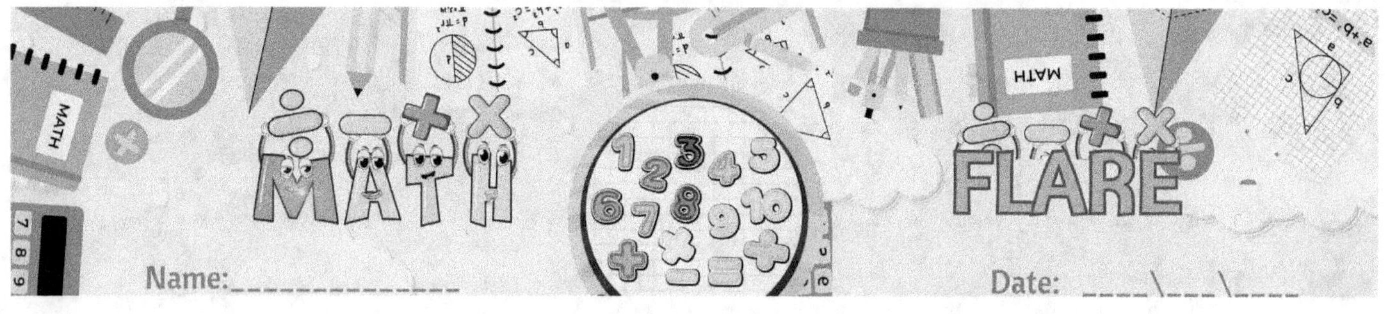

59. $(2 + 10) - (9 + 4) =$

60. $(-9) + 2 + (-7) =$

61. $1 - 3 + (-1) =$

62. $6 - (7 - 3) =$

63. $(6 - 10) + (9 + 2) =$

64. $6 - (4 - 4) =$

65. $(7 + 9) - (8 - 1) =$

66. $1 + 9 - 6 =$

67. $3 - 4 + 10 =$

68. $(-10) + 10 =$

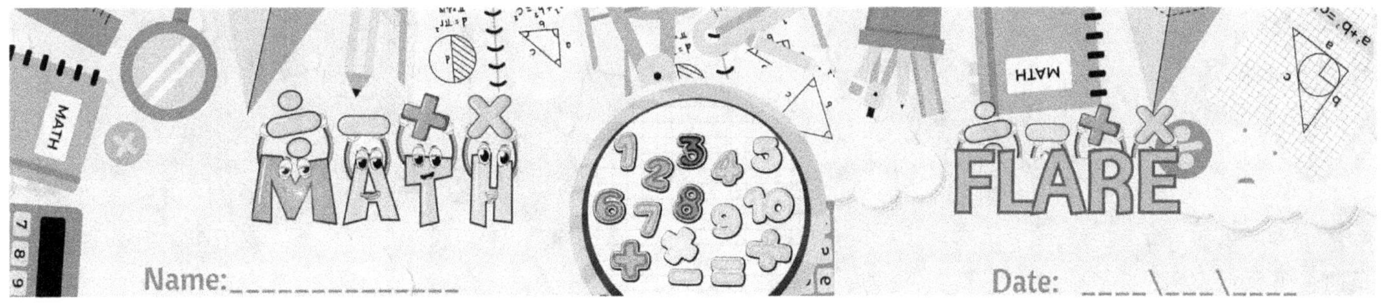

Name:_________________   Date: _____________

69. $(-2) - 5 =$

70. $8 - 2 + 5 =$

71. $(-8) + (-8) - 8 =$

72. $(9 - 7) - (8 - 8) =$

73. $(8 + 5) - 3 + 1 =$

74. $(-3) + (-8) + 9 =$

75. $8 - (-1) =$

76. $6 - (1 - 3) =$

77. $2 - 9 + 3 =$

78. $(-10) + (-6) + 4 =$

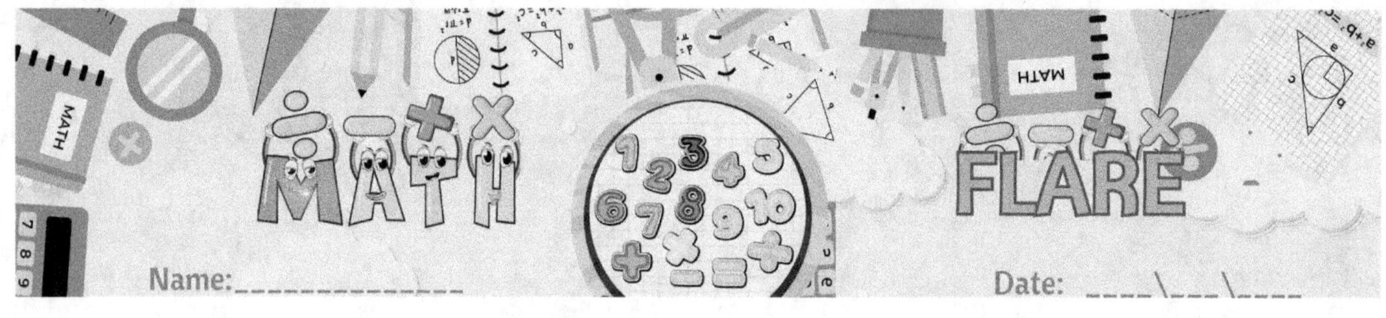

79. $(8 + 4) + (1 - 6) =$

80. $5 + (-8) + 9 =$

81. $8 - 4 + 4 =$

82. $(8 - 6) + 6 - 1 =$

83. $2 - 1 - (3 + 6) =$

84. $7 - 6 + 10 =$

85. $6 - (2 + 3) + 10 =$

86. $7 + (-4) =$

87. $(5 - 1) - (7 + 5) =$

88. $9 + (-2) - 5 =$

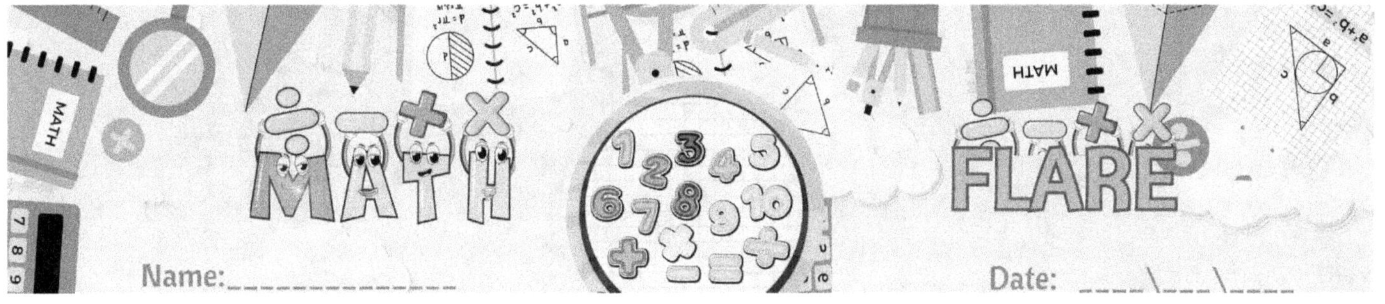

89. $10 - 5 + 8 =$

90. $(-3) + (-10) + 5 =$

91. $(-3) + 5 =$

92. $(5 - 5) - (10 + 5) =$

93. $10 - (1 + 2) - 1 =$

94. $(6 - 8) + 3 - 1 =$

95. $(-4) - 2 + (-2) =$

96. $(-9) - (-7) + 8 =$

97. $4 + (-4) - 8 =$

98. $7 - (9 + 10) - 5 =$

Name:_________________   Date: _______________

Proportional Relationship

99. $\dfrac{1}{} = \dfrac{9}{72}$

100. $\dfrac{1}{} = \dfrac{8}{88}$

101. $\dfrac{3}{4} = \dfrac{15}{}$

102. $\dfrac{2}{6} = \dfrac{16}{}$

103. $\dfrac{1}{6} = \dfrac{}{12}$

104. $\dfrac{5}{} = \dfrac{30}{54}$

105. $\dfrac{2}{11} = \dfrac{}{55}$

106. $\dfrac{1}{} = \dfrac{3}{6}$

107. $\dfrac{4}{} = \dfrac{32}{64}$

108. $\dfrac{1}{5} = \dfrac{3}{}$

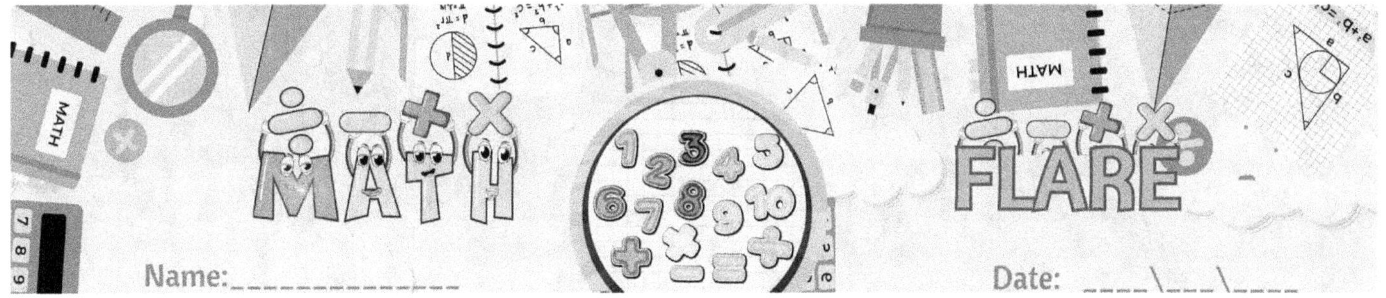

109. $\dfrac{1}{} = \dfrac{2}{6}$

110. $\dfrac{}{10} = \dfrac{30}{60}$

111. $\dfrac{9}{12} = \dfrac{90}{}$

112. $\dfrac{}{7} = \dfrac{20}{70}$

113. $\dfrac{4}{} = \dfrac{20}{60}$

114. $\dfrac{}{9} = \dfrac{48}{54}$

115. $\dfrac{}{3} = \dfrac{9}{27}$

116. $\dfrac{}{5} = \dfrac{16}{20}$

117. $\dfrac{1}{6} = \dfrac{5}{}$

118. $\dfrac{}{7} = \dfrac{10}{70}$

119. $\dfrac{8}{} = \dfrac{56}{77}$

120. $\dfrac{}{10} = \dfrac{9}{30}$

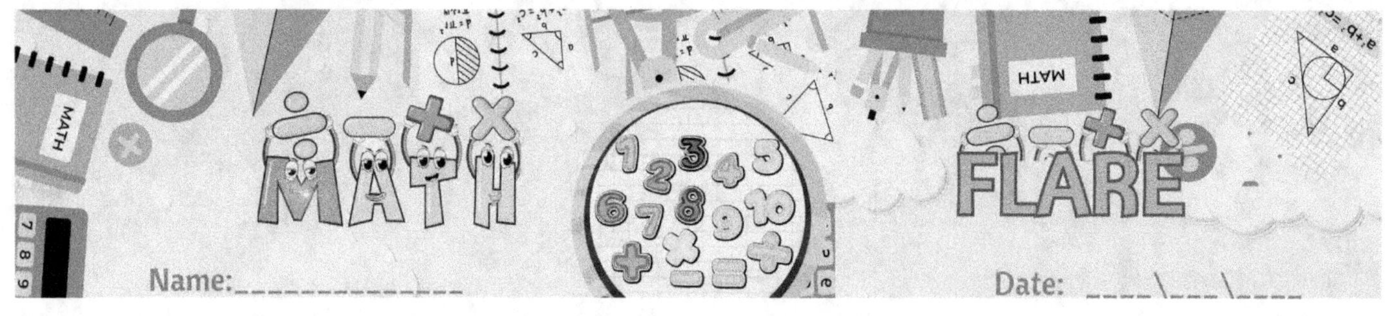

121. $\dfrac{}{8} = \dfrac{49}{56}$

122. $\dfrac{2}{4} = \dfrac{}{28}$

123. $\dfrac{2}{9} = \dfrac{10}{}$

124. $\dfrac{1}{6} = \dfrac{10}{}$

125. $\dfrac{}{10} = \dfrac{63}{70}$

126. $\dfrac{8}{11} = \dfrac{}{44}$

127. $\dfrac{}{8} = \dfrac{42}{56}$

128. $\dfrac{2}{3} = \dfrac{}{21}$

129. $\dfrac{}{4} = \dfrac{8}{32}$

130. $\dfrac{1}{2} = \dfrac{2}{}$

131. $\dfrac{}{12} = \dfrac{33}{36}$

132. $\dfrac{3}{} = \dfrac{21}{49}$

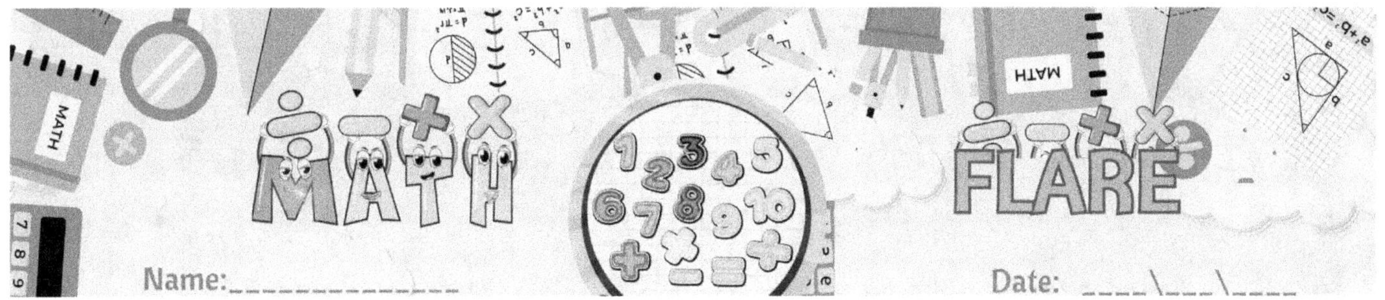

133. $\dfrac{4}{} = \dfrac{28}{35}$

134. $\dfrac{}{8} = \dfrac{16}{32}$

135. $\dfrac{1}{3} = \dfrac{}{9}$

136. $\dfrac{}{7} = \dfrac{35}{49}$

137. $\dfrac{9}{} = \dfrac{90}{110}$

138. $\dfrac{1}{2} = \dfrac{}{18}$

139. $\dfrac{}{9} = \dfrac{32}{72}$

140. $\dfrac{2}{4} = \dfrac{}{16}$

141. $\dfrac{}{12} = \dfrac{18}{108}$

142. $\dfrac{1}{10} = \dfrac{}{70}$

143. $\dfrac{1}{11} = \dfrac{9}{}$

144. $\dfrac{1}{} = \dfrac{7}{21}$

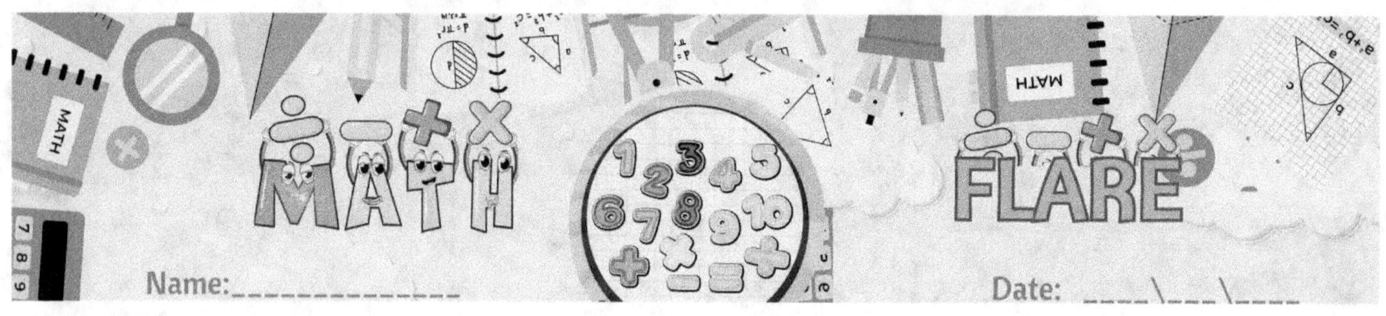

145. $\dfrac{6}{} = \dfrac{54}{72}$

146. $\dfrac{}{12} = \dfrac{42}{84}$

147. $\dfrac{}{4} = \dfrac{3}{12}$

148. $\dfrac{}{6} = \dfrac{6}{18}$

149. $\dfrac{3}{} = \dfrac{12}{36}$

150. $\dfrac{4}{5} = \dfrac{40}{}$

151. $\dfrac{5}{10} = \dfrac{}{40}$

152. $\dfrac{}{7} = \dfrac{9}{21}$

153. $\dfrac{}{2} = \dfrac{5}{10}$

154. $\dfrac{5}{} = \dfrac{15}{36}$

155. $\dfrac{}{6} = \dfrac{6}{36}$

156. $\dfrac{2}{} = \dfrac{14}{35}$

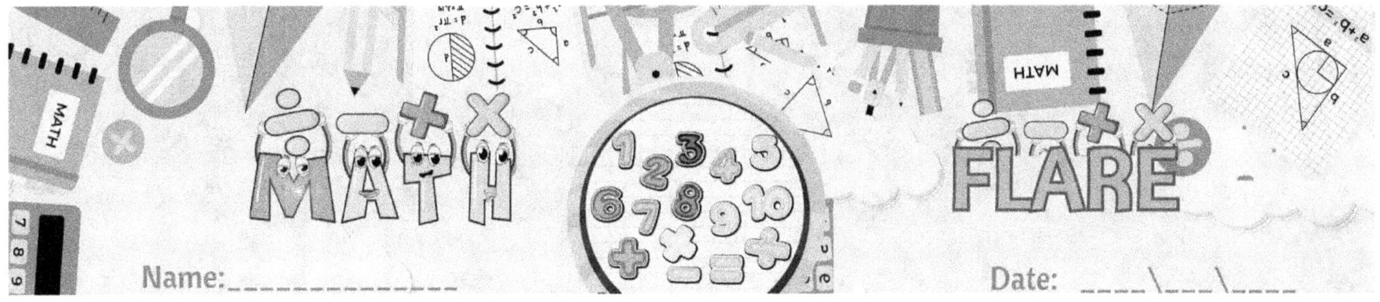

157. $\dfrac{7}{10} = \dfrac{}{50}$

158. $\dfrac{2}{8} = \dfrac{}{48}$

159. $\dfrac{1}{3} = \dfrac{}{24}$

160. $\dfrac{2}{} = \dfrac{18}{81}$

161. $\dfrac{2}{4} = \dfrac{}{32}$

162. $\dfrac{3}{} = \dfrac{24}{56}$

163. $\dfrac{3}{} = \dfrac{27}{36}$

164. $\dfrac{1}{} = \dfrac{9}{63}$

165. $\dfrac{8}{12} = \dfrac{32}{}$

166. $\dfrac{}{10} = \dfrac{50}{100}$

167. $\dfrac{4}{11} = \dfrac{}{99}$

168. $\dfrac{1}{5} = \dfrac{2}{}$

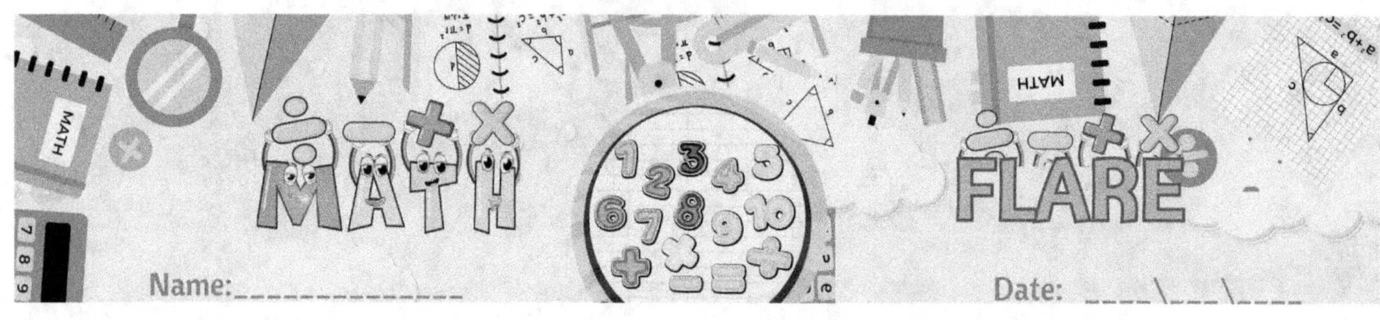

169. $\dfrac{5}{8} = \dfrac{40}{}$

170. $\dfrac{2}{6} = \dfrac{}{30}$

171. $\dfrac{7}{8} = \dfrac{21}{}$

172. $\dfrac{8}{9} = \dfrac{16}{}$

173. $\dfrac{4}{5} = \dfrac{}{30}$

174. $\dfrac{3}{12} = \dfrac{6}{}$

175. $\dfrac{6}{11} = \dfrac{30}{}$

176. $\dfrac{5}{7} = \dfrac{25}{}$

177. $\dfrac{5}{6} = \dfrac{15}{}$

178. $\dfrac{6}{10} = \dfrac{}{100}$

179. $\dfrac{2}{} = \dfrac{8}{12}$

180. $\dfrac{1}{2} = \dfrac{}{12}$

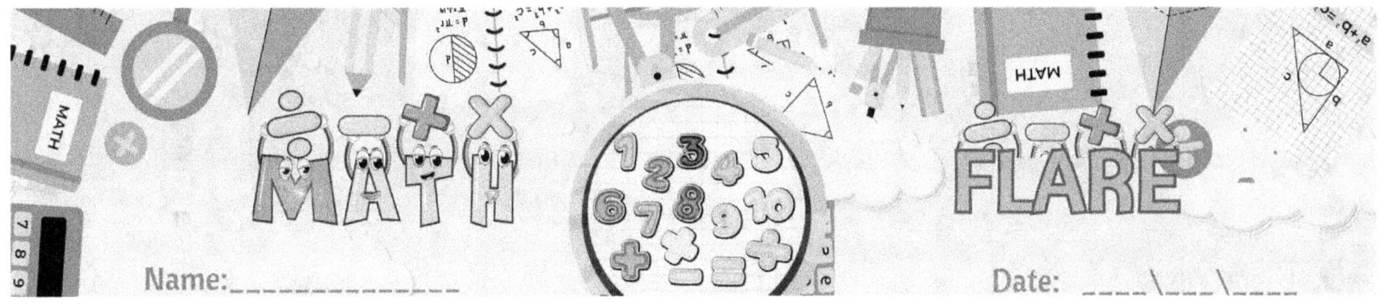

181. $\dfrac{}{8} = \dfrac{10}{80}$

182. $\dfrac{5}{7} = \dfrac{45}{}$

183. $\dfrac{}{11} = \dfrac{80}{88}$

184. $\dfrac{}{12} = \dfrac{10}{24}$

185. $\dfrac{}{3} = \dfrac{6}{18}$

186. $\dfrac{4}{} = \dfrac{20}{25}$

187. $\dfrac{3}{} = \dfrac{30}{60}$

188. $\dfrac{}{9} = \dfrac{15}{45}$

189. $\dfrac{6}{10} = \dfrac{}{20}$

190. $\dfrac{6}{8} = \dfrac{12}{}$

191. $\dfrac{}{2} = \dfrac{8}{16}$

192. $\dfrac{2}{} = \dfrac{4}{8}$

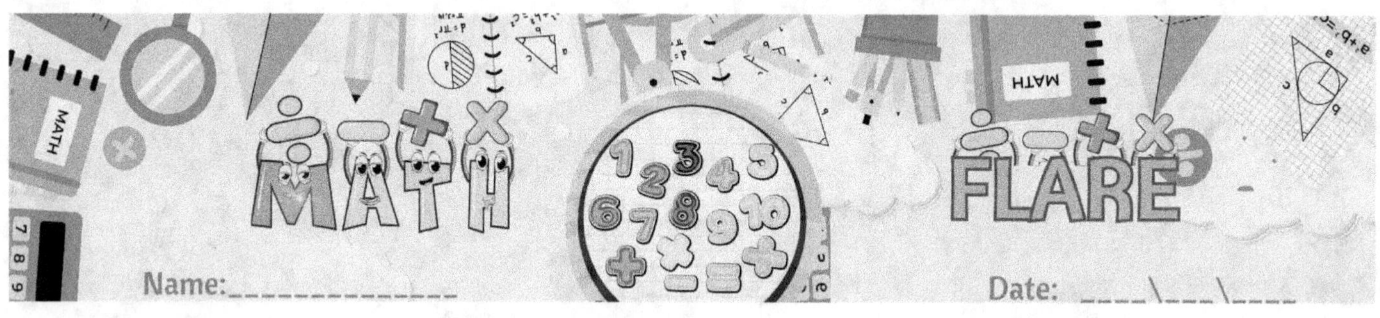

Percentage

Find the percentage of given numbers and percent values.

193. 7% of 200 = ☐

194. 3% of ☐ = 24

195. 35% of 200 = ☐

196. 10% of 800 = ☐

197. 50% of 400 = ☐

198. 8% of 100 = ☐

199. 70% of 900 = ☐

200. ☐ of 800 = 16

201. ☐ of 500 = 400

202. ☐ of 600 = 24

203. ☐ of 400 = 32

204. 7% of ☐ = 42

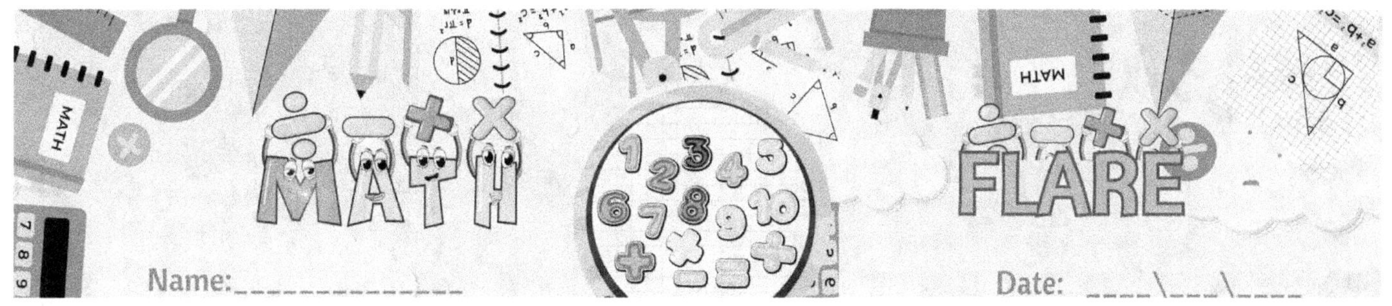

205. 60% of 300 = ☐

206. 9% of 800 = ☐

207. 75% of ☐ = 375

208. 25% of ☐ = 125

209. 10% of 900 = ☐

210. ☐ of 700 = 490

211. 80% of 400 = ☐

212. ☐ of 800 = 8

213. 35% of 40 = ☐

214. 200% of ☐ = 1800

215. 300% of 600 = ☐

216. 20% of ☐ = 20

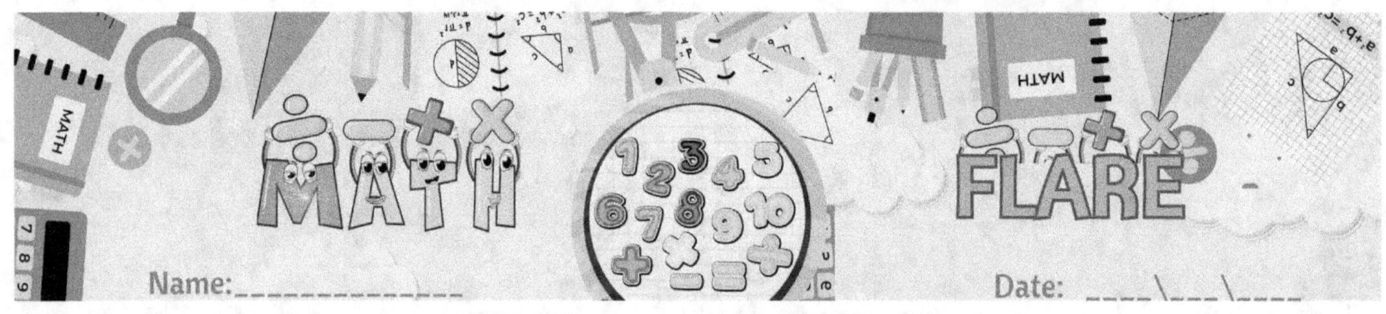

217. 30% of 600 = ☐

218. ☐ of 500 = 450

219. 3% of 700 = ☐

220. ☐ of 600 = 240

221. 6% of 900 = ☐

222. 50% of 200 = ☐

223. ☐ of 400 = 60

224. ☐ of 400 = 20

225. 100% of 200 = ☐

226. 2% of ☐ = 4

227. ☐ of 900 = 270

228. ☐ of 500 = 175

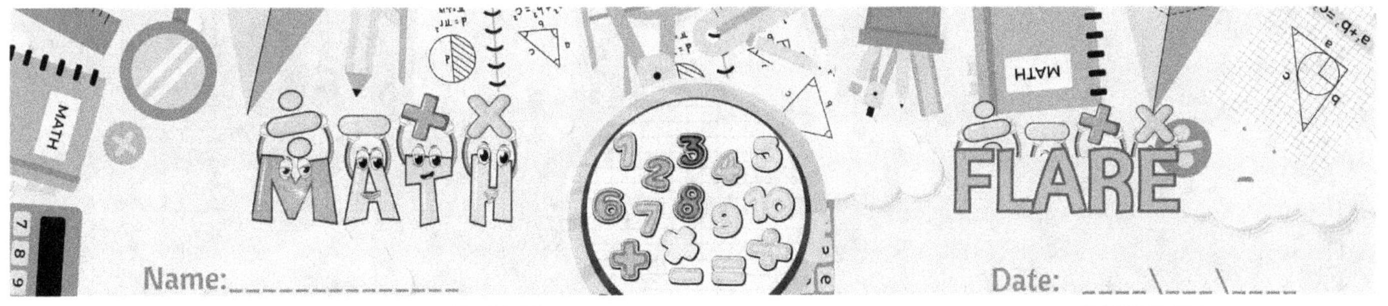

229. 80% of 50 = ☐

230. 50% of 900 = ☐

231. ☐ of 90 = 2.7

232. 25% of 400 = ☐

233. ☐ of 700 = 700

234. ☐ of 400 = 160

235. ☐ of 300 = 24

236. 300% of ☐ = 210

237. 200% of 500 = ☐

238. ☐ of 800 = 160

239. 2% of ☐ = 10

240. 60% of 800 = ☐

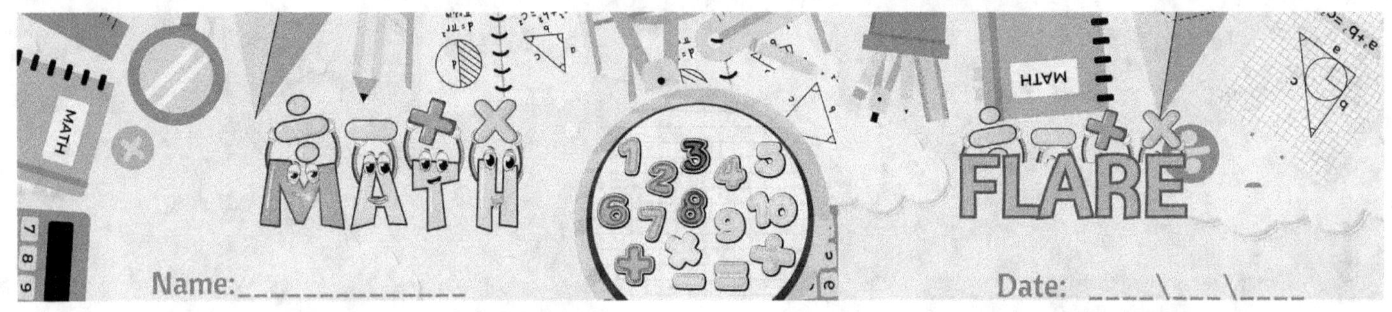

241. 90% of 300 = ☐

242. 4% of 700 = ☐

243. 75% of 700 = ☐

244. ☐ of 200 = 10

245. ☐ of 200 = 30

246. ☐ of 90 = 6.3

247. 1% of 200 = ☐

248. 1% of ☐ = 9

249. 9% of ☐ = 27

250. ☐ of 800 = 640

251. ☐ of 100 = 35

252. 75% of ☐ = 675

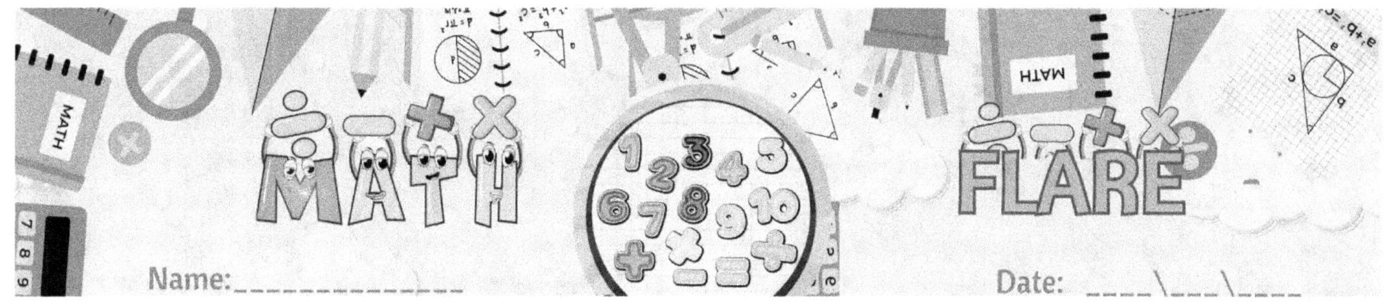

253. [ ] of 300 = 18

254. 50% of [ ] = 45

255. [ ] of 900 = 36

256. [ ] of 400 = 120

257. [ ] of 900 = 360

258. 25% of 600 = [ ]

259. 300% of [ ] = 1200

260. 10% of [ ] = 40

261. 70% of 200 = [ ]

262. 3% of [ ] = 12

263. 20% of 30 = [ ]

264. 8% of 40 = [ ]

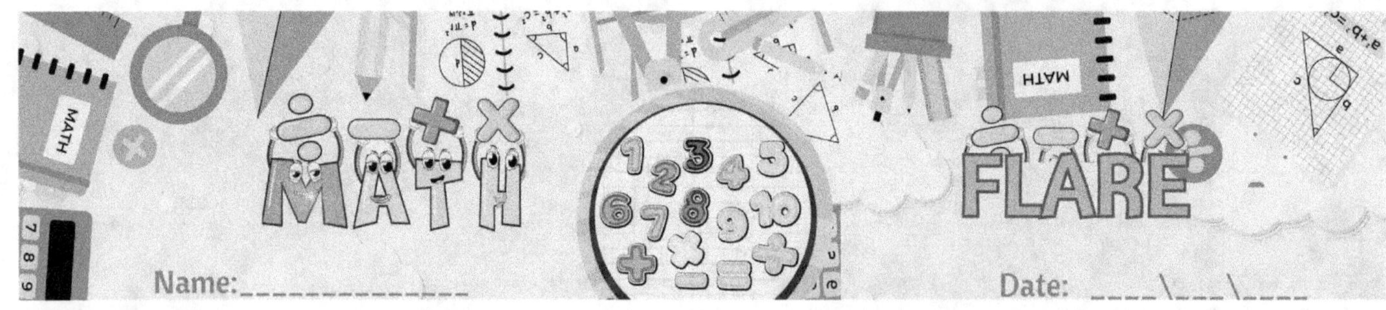

265. 2% of 600 = ▢

266. 200% of 200 = ▢

267. 5% of 800 = ▢

268. 90% of ▢ = 90

269. 8% of ▢ = 56

270. 20% of ▢ = 60

271. 3% of 600 = ▢

272. 6% of 700 = ▢

273. 4% of 100 = ▢

274. 15% of 500 = ▢

275. 30% of ▢ = 30

276. ▢ of 100 = 100

277. 7% of 100 = ☐

278. 70% of 100 = ☐

279. ☐ of 700 = 35

280. 35% of 900 = ☐

281. 75% of ☐ = 75

282. 10% of 200 = ☐

283. 80% of 600 = ☐

284. 7% of ☐ = 56

285. 5% of 900 = ☐

286. 15% of ☐ = 9

287. 90% of 200 = ☐

288. 9% of ☐ = 9

289. 75% of 400 = ☐

290. 35% of 300 = ☐

291. 1% of ☐ = 3

292. 6% of 800 = ☐

293. 36.9% of 747 = ☐

294. ☐ of 91 = 1.365

295. 0.7% of 9 = ☐

296. 4.9% of 6 = ☐

297. ☐ of 3 = 0.165

298. 11.6% of 80 = ☐

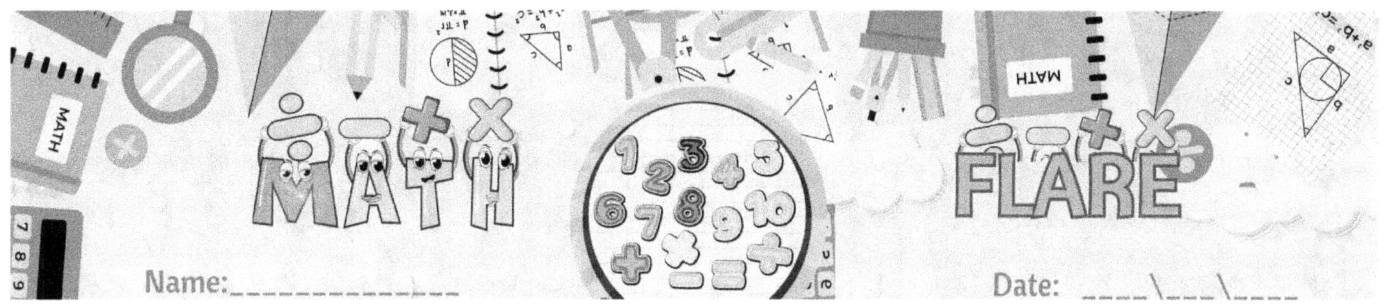

299. 4.5% of ☐ = 0.09

300. 32.0% of ☐ = 16.64

301. 4.2% of 341 = ☐

302. ☐ of 33 = 9.471

303. 8.9% of ☐ = 0.178

304. 4.8% of 52 = ☐

305. ☐ of 158 = 0.316

306. ☐ of 664 = 35.192

307. 6.8% of 785 = ☐

308. ☐ of 151 = 25.972

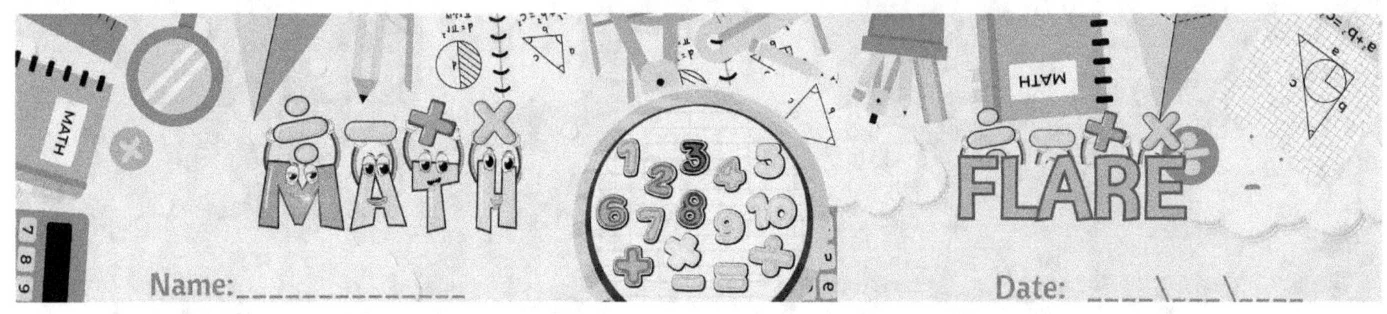

309. [ ] of 199 = 1.393

310. 9.8% of [ ] = 54.194

311. 5.5% of 6 = [ ]

312. [ ] of 491 = 3.437

313. 10.2% of 4 = [ ]

314. 48.8% of 14 = [ ]

315. [ ] of 66 = 0.396

316. [ ] of 24 = 11.856

317. [ ] of 66 = 6.204

318. 0.5% of 245 = [ ]

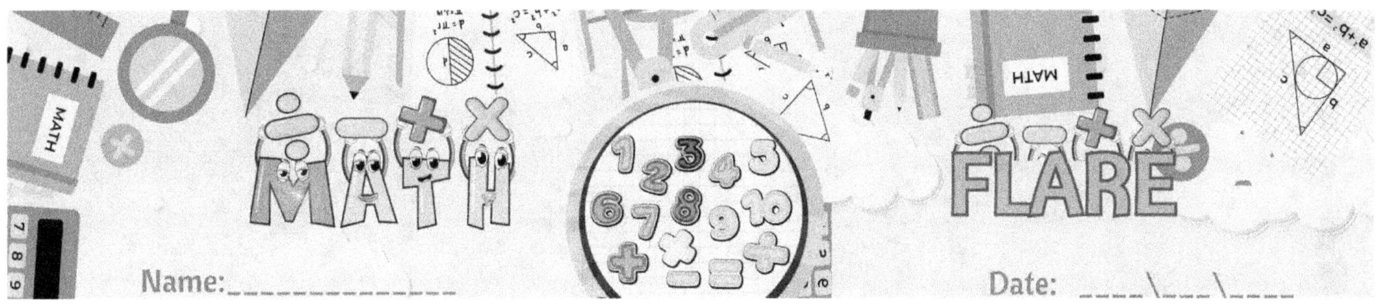

319. 0.6% of ☐ = 5.31

320. 0.7% of ☐ = 5.334

321. ☐ of 1 = 0.098

322. 8.4% of 9 = ☐

323. ☐ of 6 = 0.036

324. 9.8% of ☐ = 4.606

325. 0.3% of 37 = ☐

326. ☐ of 921 = 339.849

327. ☐ of 8 = 0.12

328. 0.7% of 32 = ☐

Name:_________________ Date: ____________

329. 4.9% of ⬚ = 0.098

330. 5.5% of ⬚ = 0.385

331. 11.6% of ⬚ = 4.872

332. ⬚ of 65 = 20.8

333. 4.2% of ⬚ = 17.136

334. ⬚ of 706 = 202.622

335. 8.9% of 1 = ⬚

336. 4.8% of ⬚ = 0.096

337. 0.2% of ⬚ = 0.002

338. ⬚ of 99 = 5.247

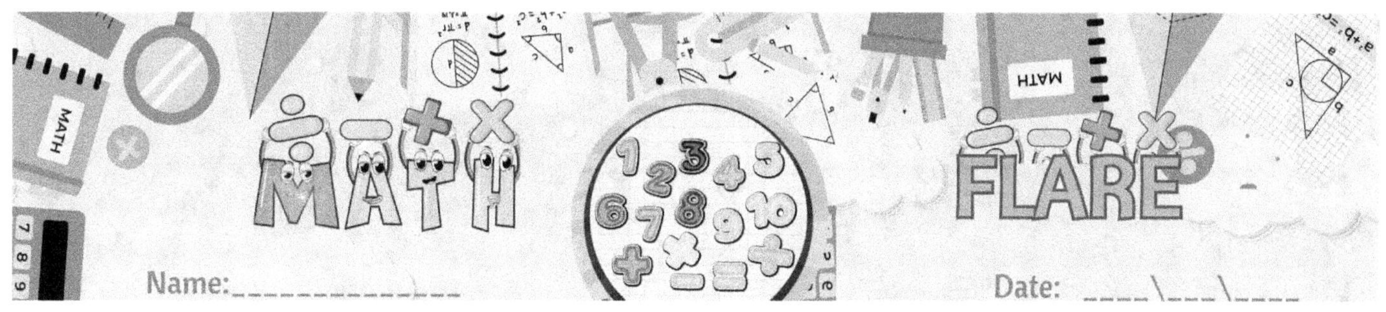

339. [   ] of 6 = 0.408

340. [   ] of 188 = 32.336

341. 0.7% of 16 = [   ]

342. 9.8% of [   ] = 60.172

343. [   ] of 839 = 46.145

344. [   ] of 6 = 0.042

345. 10.2% of [   ] = 86.7

346. 48.8% of [   ] = 78.08

347. 0.6% of 9 = [   ]

348. 49.4% of 209 = [   ]

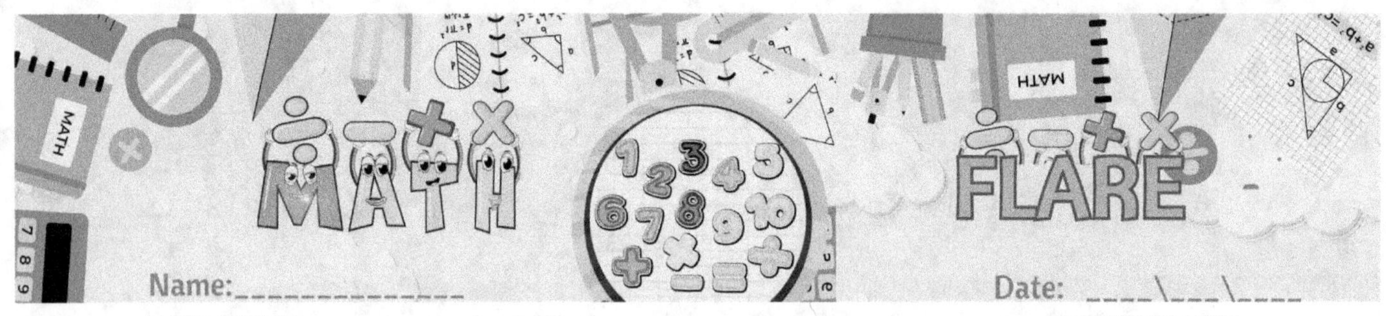

349. [____] of 59 = 5.546

350. 0.5% of 36 = [____]

351. 0.6% of [____] = 0.438

352. [____] of 8 = 0.056

353. 9.8% of [____] = 1.96

354. [____] of 45 = 3.78

355. [____] of 352 = 2.112

356. 9.8% of 556 = [____]

357. 0.3% of 535 = [____]

358. [____] of 120 = 44.28

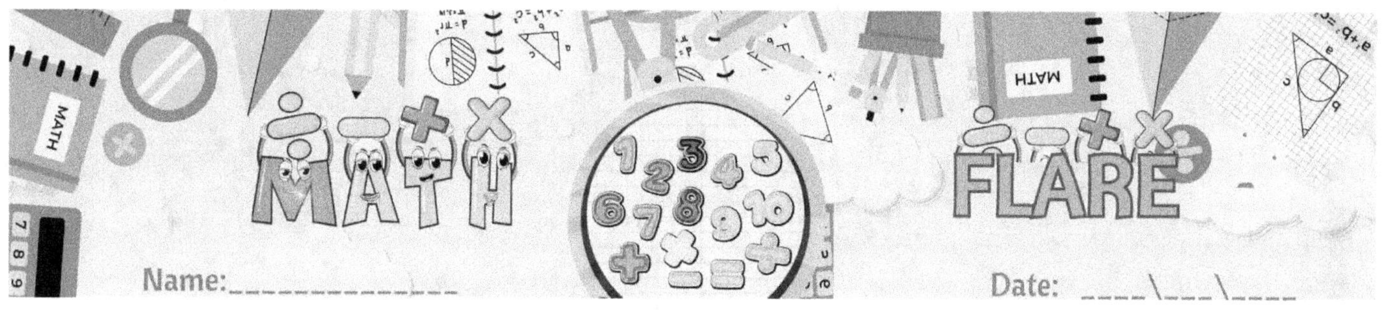

Convert Percent and Decimals

359. $38\% = $ _______________

360. $0.67 = $ _______________

361. $83\% = $ _______________

362. $0.92 = $ _______________

363. $75\% = $ _______________

364. $0.98 = $ _______________

365. $0.51 = $ _______________

366. $0.27 = $ _______________

367. $41\% = $ _______________

368. $74\% = $ _______________

369. $91\% = $ _______________

370. $0.08 = $ _______________

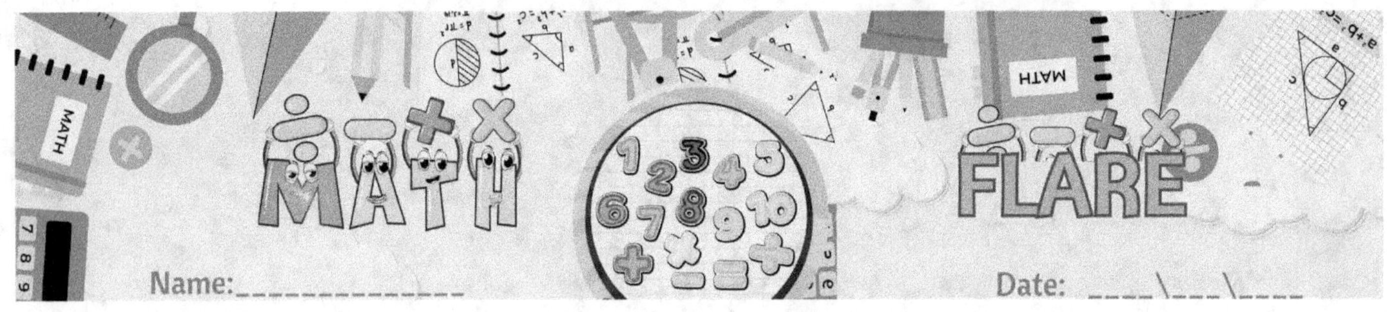

371. 89 % = ___________________

372. 4 % = ___________________

373. 44 % = ___________________

374. 18 % = ___________________

375. 9 % = ___________________

376. 34 % = ___________________

377. 7 % = ___________________

378. 0.6 = ___________________

379. 82 % = ___________________

380. 0.93 = ___________________

381. 0.02 = ___________________

382. 0.19 = ___________________

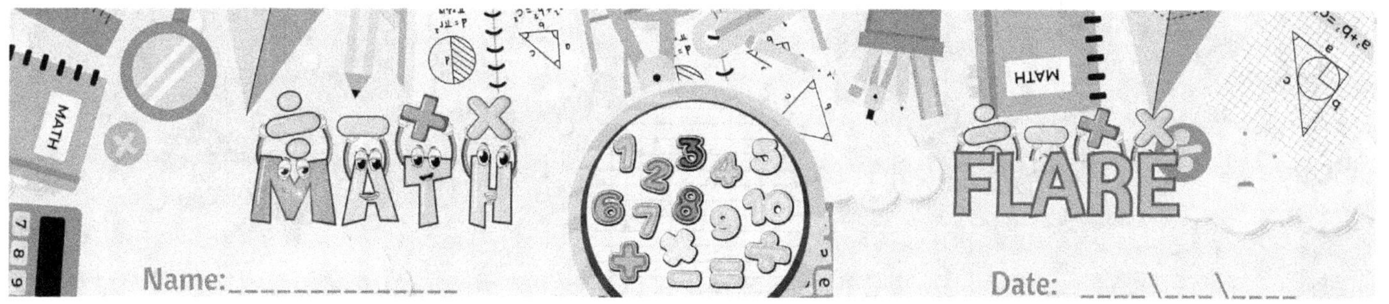

383. 0.24 = _______________

384. 0.66 = _______________

385. 0.94 = _______________

386. 0.33 = _______________

387. 0.84 = _______________

388. 69 % = _______________

389. 59 % = _______________

390. 0.88 = _______________

391. 0.7 = _______________

392. 43 % = _______________

393. 72 % = _______________

394. 80 % = _______________

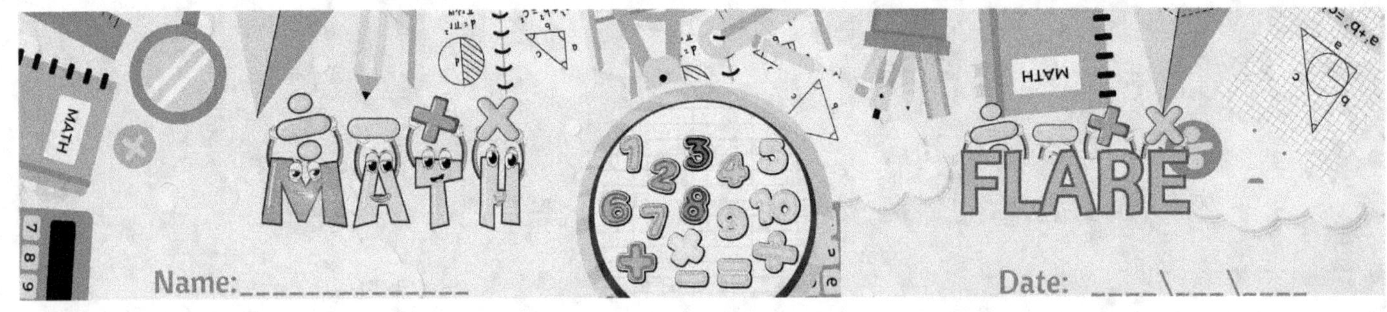

395. 54 % = _______________

396. 61 % = _______________

397. 96 % = _______________

398. 97 % = _______________

399. 12 % = _______________

400. 0.25 = _______________

401. 0.01 = _______________

402. 0.99 = _______________

403. 0.57 = _______________

404. 79 % = _______________

405. 0.29 = _______________

406. 0.03 = _______________

407. 0.42 = _______________

408. 0.39 = _______________

409. 31 % = _______________

410. 56 % = _______________

411. 48 % = _______________

412. 0.21 = _______________

413. 1 = _______________

414. 65 % = _______________

415. 95 % = _______________

416. 81 % = _______________

417. 73 % = _______________

418. 87 % = _______________

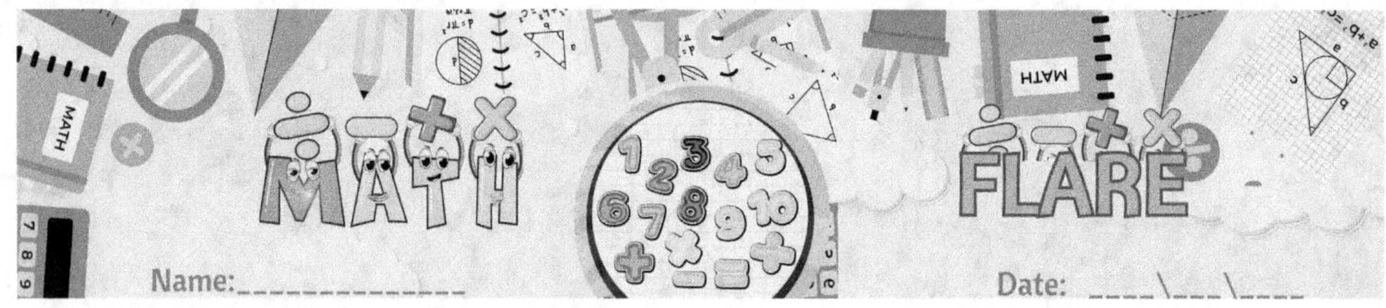

Word Problems: Percent

419. A school has 50 students. If 16% of them play baseball, how many students play baseball?

420. A company wants to increase its revenue by 35%. If its current revenue is $80.00 million, what should be its new revenue?

421. A store has 100 cotton swabs. If 6% of them are sold at the end of the day, how many cotton swabs are sold?

422. Owen earned $50.00 for a week's work. If he paid 16% of it in taxes how much did he pay in taxes?

Name:_______________   Date: _____________

423. A store is having a sale where everything is 25% off. The soaps originally priced at $4.00 is now on sale. How much is the new price of soaps now?

424. Sadie bought erasers for $20.00. If she paid an additional 25% for sales tax, how much in total did she pay for the erasers?

425. In a class of 80 students, 35% of them are in the Math Club. How many students are in the Math Club?

426. Aaliyah bought a shoes for $60.00. If she paid an additional 5% for sales tax, how much in total did she pay for the shoes?

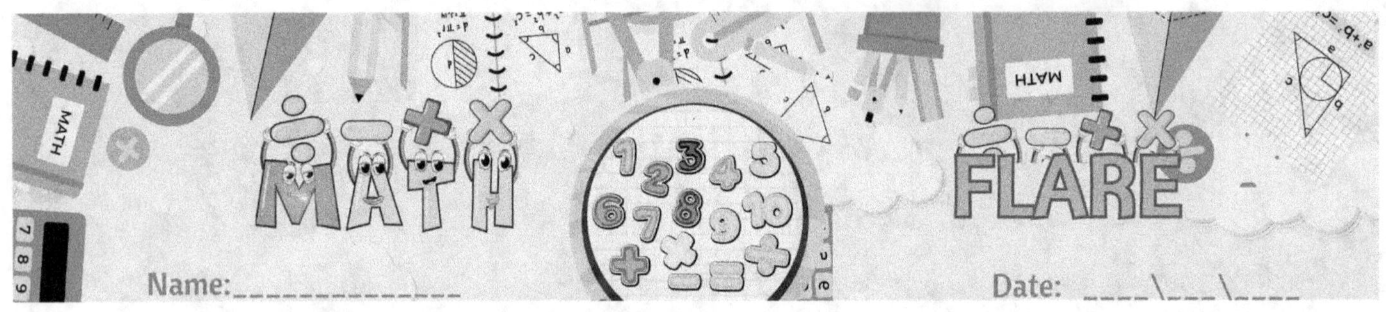

427. Gabriel buys thermometers for $20.00 to sell them in market. If he wants to earn 5% profit. What must be the selling price of thermometers?

428. Benjamin had 100 bandages. He gave away 6% of them. How many did he have left?

429. In a school of 50 students, 46% of them take the bus to school. How many students take the bus?

430. Logan's monthly sales of toothbrushes was $76.00. If he earned 25% of profit, what was his profit?

431. In a class of 56 students, 25% are girls. How many are girls?

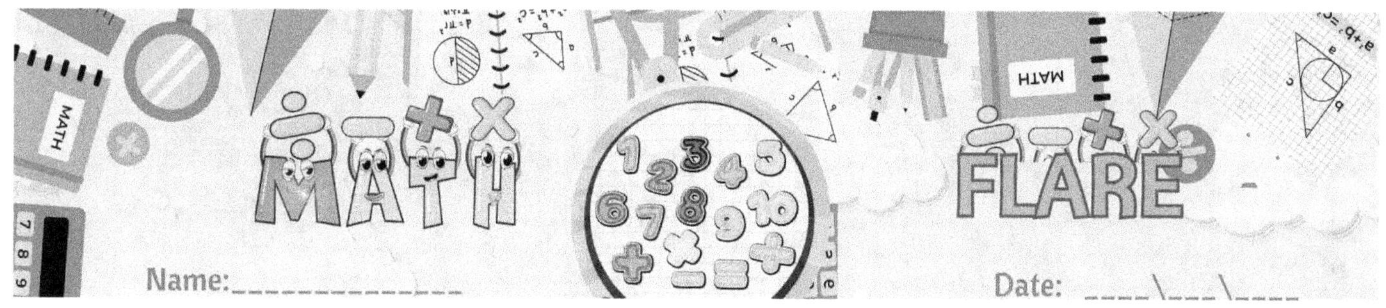

432. A store offers 25% discount on all products. If the original price of breads was 44, what is the sales price?

433. A school has 8 students. If 25% of them play tennis, how many students play tennis?

434. Hailey had a collection of 80 baseball cards. She gave away 5% of them. How many did she have left?

435. In a basket of 75 microphones, 24% are red microphones . How many are red microphones?

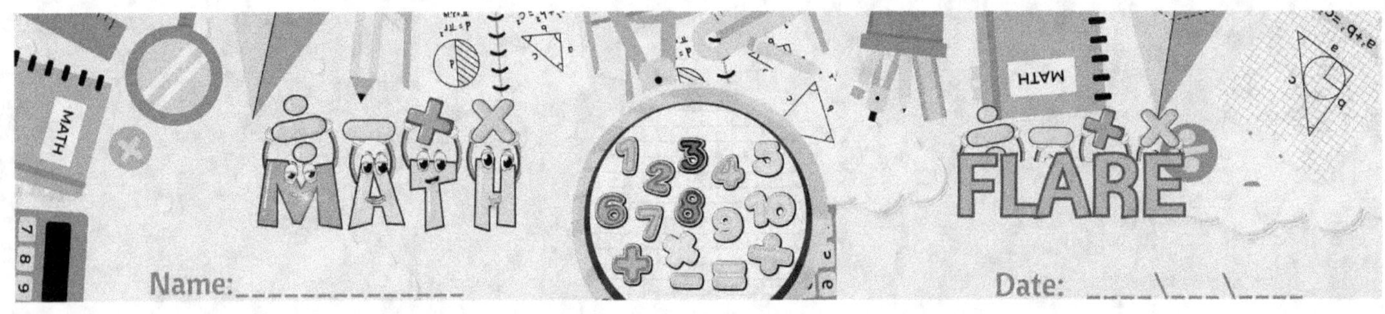

436. Miles bought a bicycle that cost $40.00 when it was new. If he eventually sold it for 25% of the original cost, how much was it sold for?

437. In a survey of 40 people, 5% said they prefer cats over dogs. How many people prefer cats?

438. Nova bought a pizza for $100.00. If she paid an additional 1% for sales tax, how much in total did she pay for the pizza?

439. What is 25% of 72?

440. A store offers 5% discount on all products. If the sale price of shoes was 100, what was the original price?

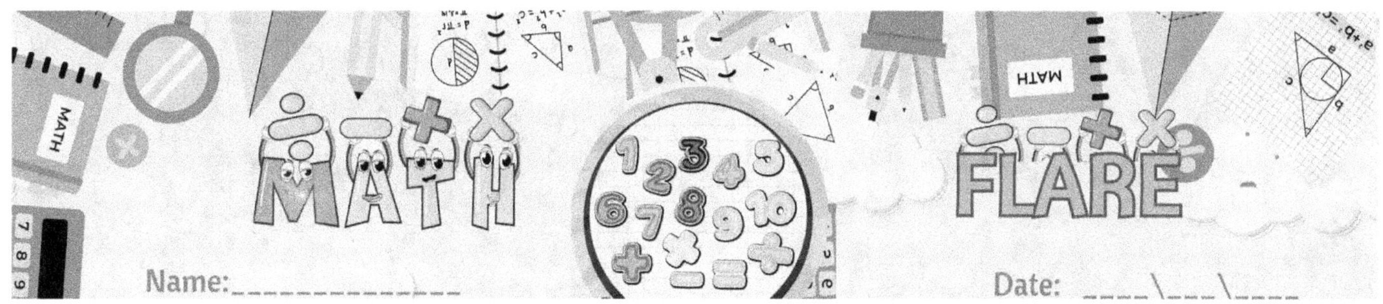

441. A store increases the prices of all items by 5%. If the needles originally costs $20.00, what is the sale price?

442. A teacher gave a math test with 8 questions. If a student got 25% questions correct, how many questions were correct?

443. A school has 50 students. If 52% of them play football, how many students play football?

444. A school has a total of 4 teachers. If 25% of them are men, how many male teachers are there?

445. Amelia bought a bag for $20.00. If she paid an additional 25% for sales tax, how much in total did she pay for the bag?

446. In a survey of 4 people, 25% said they preferred android OS. How many people preferred android OS?

447. A car dealership sold 80 cars last month. If the sales increased by 5% this month, how many cars did they sell this month?

448. If the number 40 is decreased by 5%, what is the value of the new number?

449. A school has a total of 25 teachers. If 52% of them are men, how many female teachers are there?

450. A classroom has 20 students, of which 5% are girls. How many boys are in the classroom?

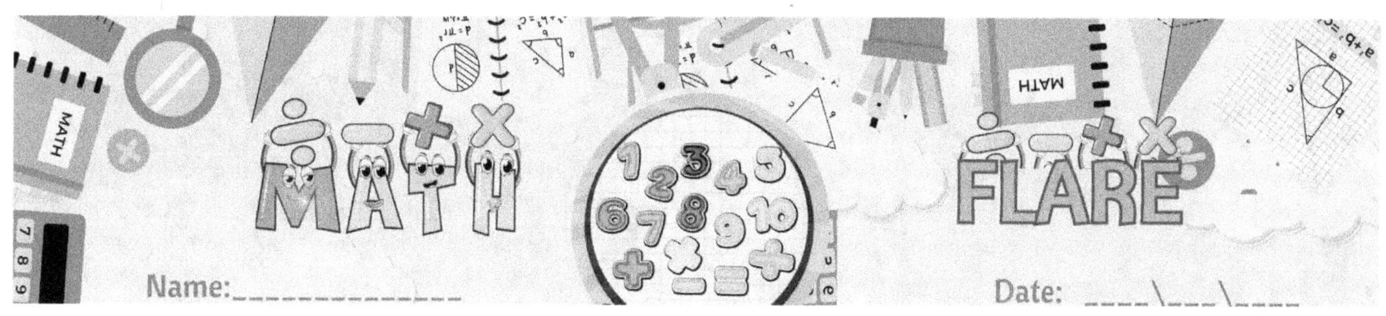

451. A restaurant makes a pizza that is 40 inches in diameter. If they want to increase the size of the pizza by 25%, what will be the new diameter?

452. A store offers a 25% discount on all items. If Isabella buys spoons originally priced at $80.00, how much money did she save?

453. In a class of 100 students, 16% are boys. How many are boys?

454. A person wants to make a 5% tip on a $100.00 meal. How much should the tip be?

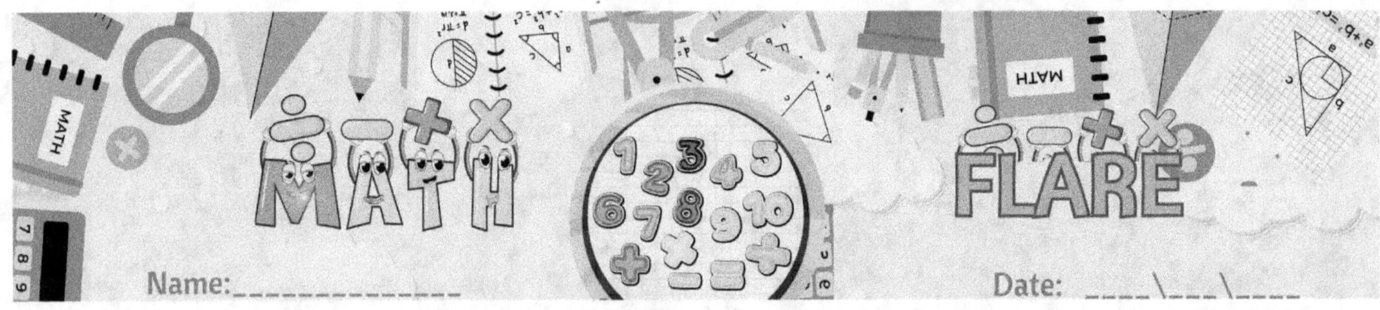

455. Everly bought a book for $4.00. If she paid an additional 25% for sales tax, how much in total did she pay for the book?

456. Aubree bought a camera for $100.00. If she paid an additional 9% for sales tax, how much in total did she pay for the camera?

457. If the number 50 is increased by 32%, what is the value of the new number?

458. Harper bought some deodorants for $50.00. If she paid an additional 16% for sales tax, how much in total did she pay for the deodorants?

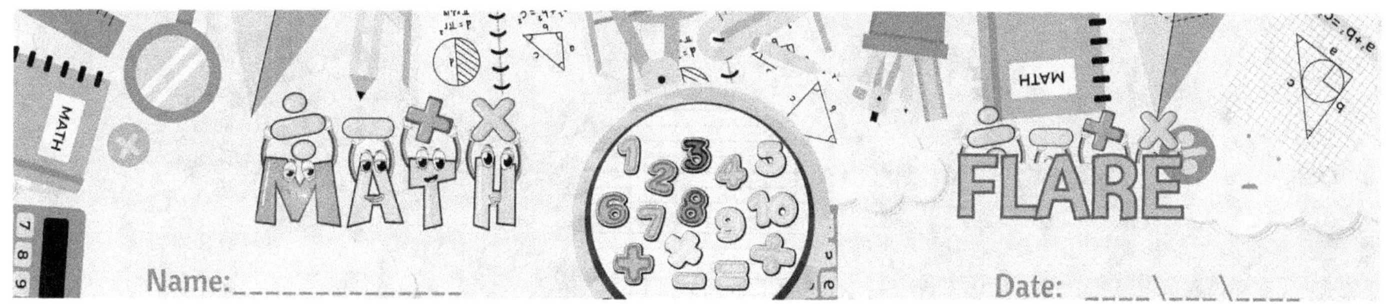

Name:________________   Date: ______________

459. A school has a total of 8 teachers. If 25% of them are men, how many female teachers are there?

460. Bella bought a book for $100.00. If she paid an additional 6% for sales tax, how much in total did she pay for the book?

461. A school has 4 students. If 25% of them play tennis, how many students play tennis?

462. Hazel bought a bag for $75.00. If she paid an additional 24% for sales tax, how much in total did she pay for the bag?

463. Peyton bought a shoes for $50.00. If she paid an additional 52% for sales tax, how much in total did she pay for the shoes?

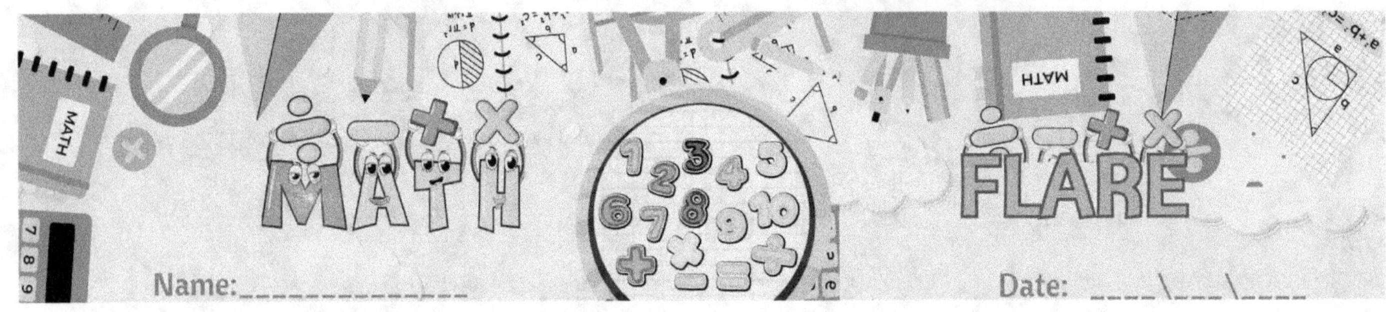

464. A school has 40 students. If 5% of them play football, how many students play football?

465. A school has 25 students. If 24% of them play baseball, how many students play baseball?

466. Grayson had 75 flowers. He gave away 84% of them. How many did he have left?

467. A person wants to make a 52% tip on a $100.00 meal. How much should the tip be?

468. Skylar bought some hats for $88.00. If she paid an additional 25% for sales tax, how much in total did she pay for the hats?

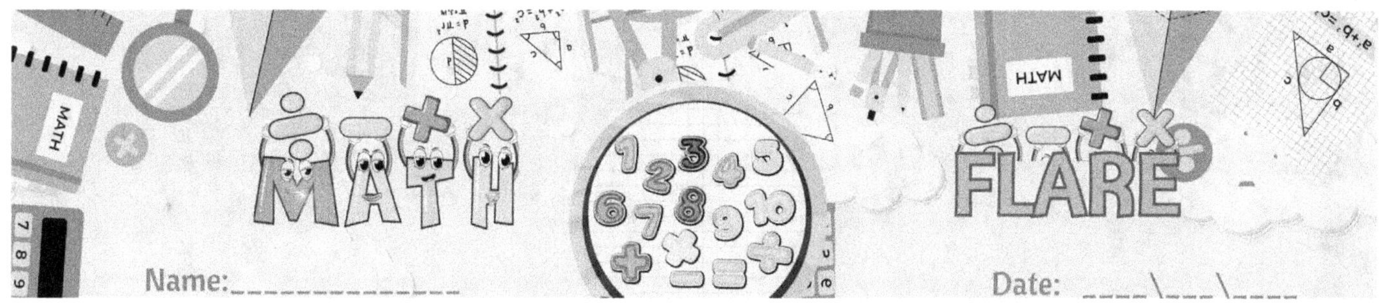

Convert: Ratio, Fraction, Percent, and Decimals

469.

	Ratio	Fraction	Percent	Decimal
a.				0.944
b.			100%	
c.	2:11			
d.		4/12		
e.				0.105
f.			14.3%	
g.				0.9
h.				0.5
i.			42.9%	
j.	12:15			
k.			29.4%	
l.		1/4		
m.				0.786
n.		3/20		
o.				0.286

470.

	Ratio	Fraction	Percent	Decimal
a.	2:8			
b.		9/14		
c.		5/7		
d.			66.7%	
e.			100%	
f.			50%	
g.			33.3%	
h.	19:20			
i.	2:7			
j.				0.143
k.	10:11			
l.				0.857
m.		2/4		
n.				0.714
o.		3/14		

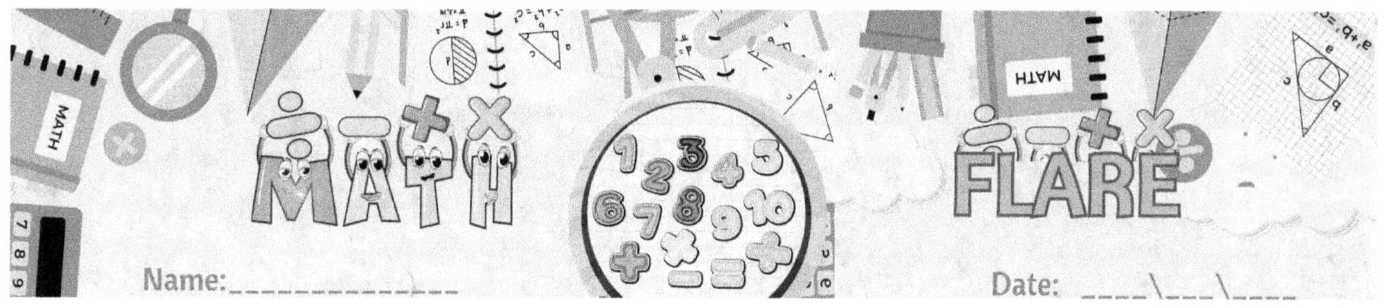

471.

	Ratio	Fraction	Percent	Decimal
a.			100%	
b.				0.5
c.			71.4%	
d.			28.6%	
e.				0.733
f.				0.2
g.	1:2			
h.	11:13			
i.	3:4			
j.			15.8%	
k.				0.588
l.				0.636
m.	2:3			
n.		2/6		
o.		5/7		

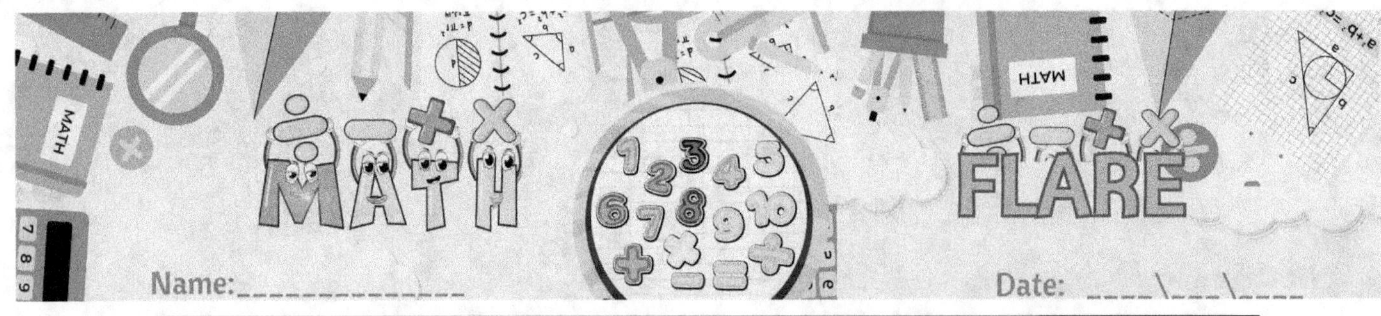

472.

	Ratio	Fraction	Percent	Decimal
a.				0.4
b.			100%	
c.	1:3			
d.				0.538
e.			66.7%	
f.				0.158
g.				0.5
h.				0.5
i.				0.188
j.		2/3		
k.			56.2%	
l.				0.875
m.	1:8			
n.				0.143
o.		1/9		

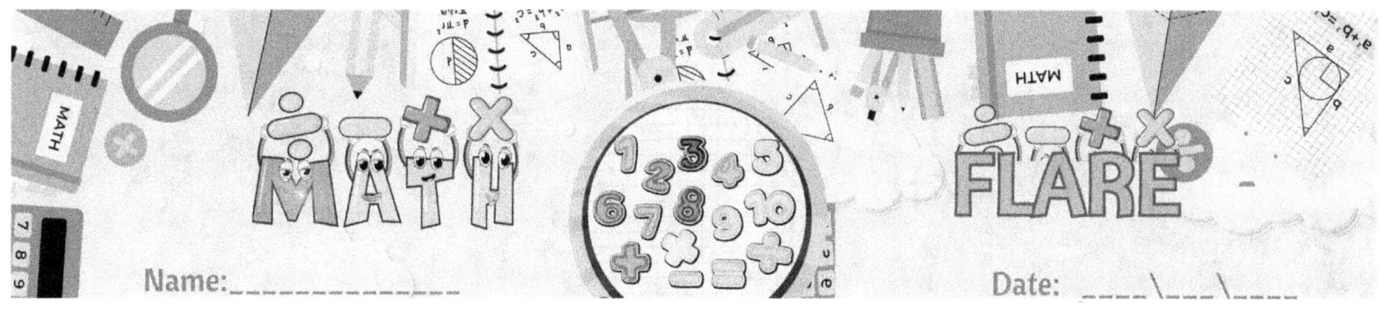

473.

	Ratio	Fraction	Percent	Decimal
a.		1/17		
b.		5/5		
c.	3:14			
d.		3/4		
e.		4/10		
f.		4/5		
g.				0.25
h.				0.7
i.			16.7%	
j.	6:10			
k.	11:12			
l.	4:11			
m.	12:18			
n.			50%	
o.	9:15			

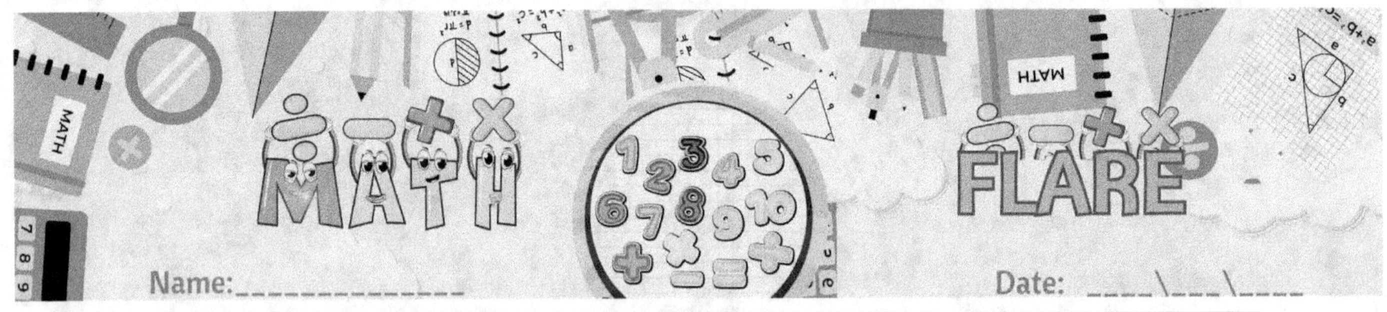

474.

	Ratio	Fraction	Percent	Decimal
a.	3:3			
b.				0.6
c.				0.5
d.				0.667
e.	4:13			
f.		2/4		
g.				0.882
h.			75%	
i.			83.3%	
j.			76.9%	
k.		6/11		
l.	3:11			
m.		9/10		
n.				0.3
o.				0.316

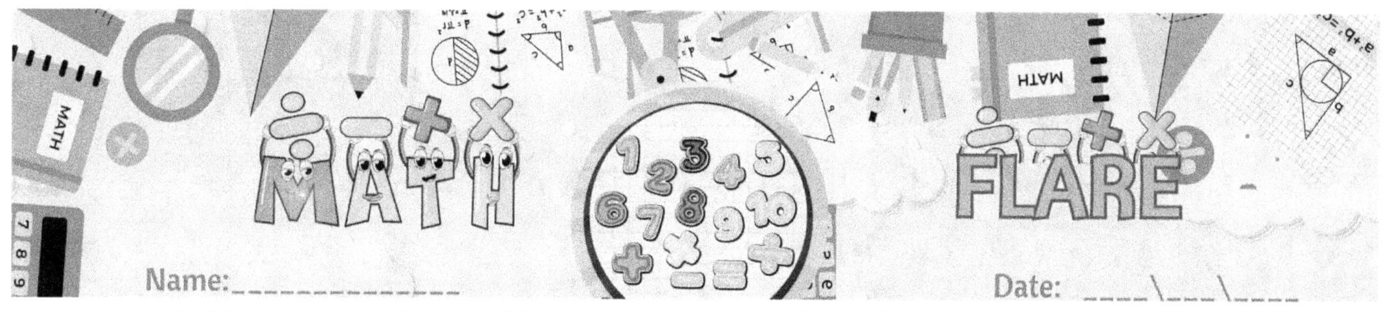

475.

	Ratio	Fraction	Percent	Decimal
a.			100%	
b.			91.7%	
c.		9/15		
d.			58.3%	
e.				0.667
f.		7/16		
g.				0.421
h.			75%	
i.	6:7			
j.	13:14			
k.	3:7			
l.	2:15			
m.		4/5		
n.		18/19		
o.				0.4

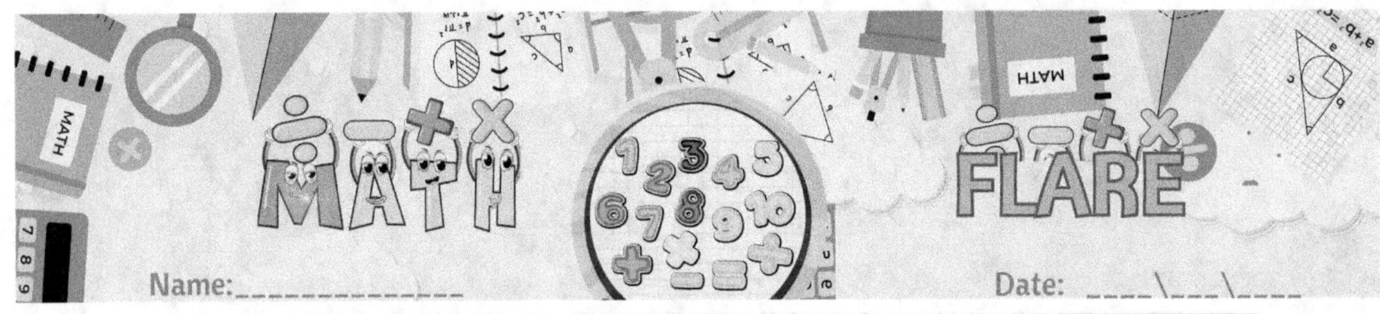

476.

	Ratio	Fraction	Percent	Decimal
a.				0.2
b.		1/1		
c.				0.059
d.		5/8		
e.	1:6			
f.	15:19			
g.			65%	
h.		5/6		
i.				0.167
j.	9:11			
k.				0.429
l.				0.214
m.	3:9			
n.				0.125
o.	2:15			

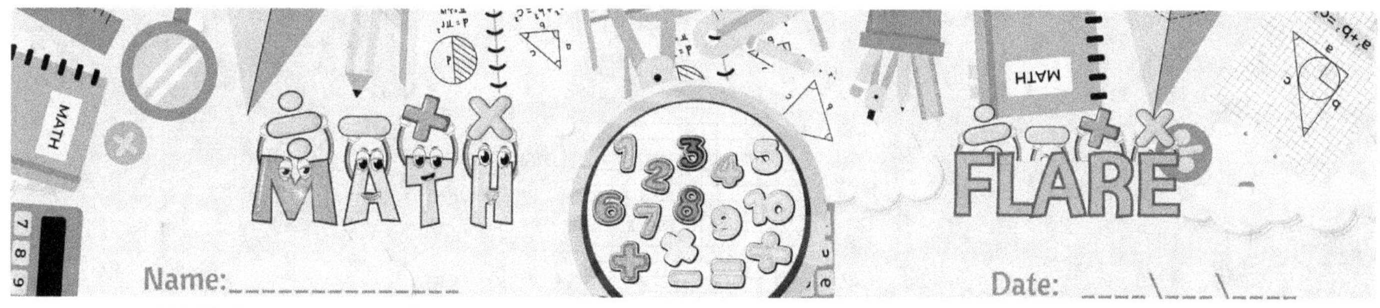

477.

	Ratio	Fraction	Percent	Decimal
a.		13/16		
b.	14:20			
c.	8:11			
d.	1:1			
e.	2:3			
f.	1:20			
g.				0.143
h.		1/2		
i.		8/17		
j.				0.882
k.		8/18		
l.				0.286
m.				0.25
n.				0.133
o.	12:18			

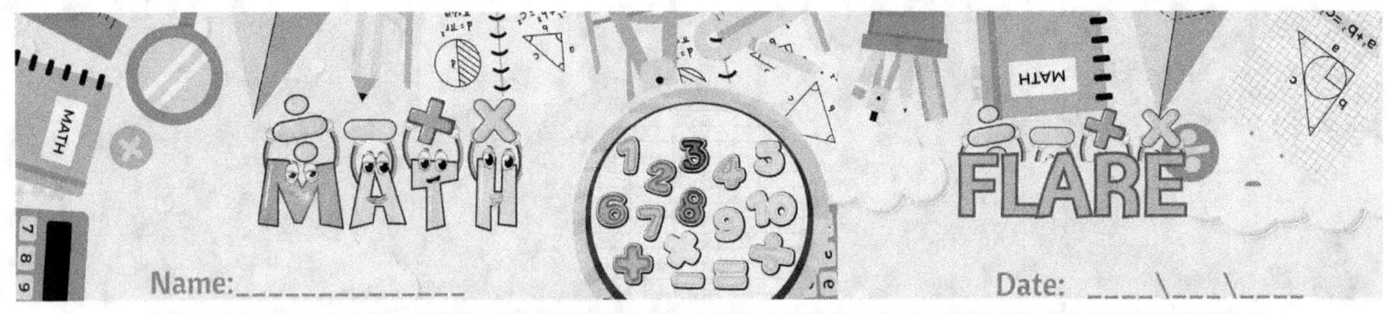

478.

	Ratio	Fraction	Percent	Decimal
a.	3:5			
b.	4:17			
c.		11/13		
d.	2:16			
e.	7:9			
f.			16.7%	
g.		8/11		
h.			100%	
i.		11/19		
j.				0.429
k.	18:19			
l.				0.2
m.			37.5%	
n.				0.833
o.			11.1%	

ANSWERS

Page 1: Positive and Negative Integers

1. -12	2. -12	3. -20	4. 5	5. 12	6. -6	7. 9
8. 9	9. 3	10. -5	11. 2	12. -1	13. -12	14. -5
15. -8	16. -1	17. -2	18. 4	19. 11	20. 0	21. -3
22. -7	23. 16	24. -12	25. -7	26. 1	27. -20	28. 14
29. -6	30. 1	31. -9	32. -3	33. -18	34. -17	35. -1
36. -9	37. 4	38. 4	39. 15	40. 2	41. -2	42. 9
43. 8	44. -13	45. 6	46. 9	47. -4	48. 6	49. -3
50. 6	51. -16	52. -10	53. 5	54. -20	55. 2	56. -9
57. 13	58. 6	59. -1	60. -14	61. -3	62. 2	63. 7
64. 6	65. 9	66. 4	67. 9	68. 0	69. -7	70. 11
71. -24	72. 2	73. 11	74. -2	75. 9	76. 8	77. -4
78. -12	79. 7	80. 6	81. 8	82. 7	83. -8	84. 11
85. 11	86. 3	87. -8	88. 2	89. 13	90. -8	91. 2
92. -15	93. 6	94. 0	95. -8	96. 6	97. -8	98. -17

Page 11: Proportional Relationship

99. 8	100. 11	101. 20	102. 48	103. 2	104. 9	105. 10
106. 2	107. 8	108. 15	109. 3	110. 5	111. 120	112. 2
113. 12	114. 8	115. 1	116. 4	117. 30	118. 1	119. 11
120. 3	121. 7	122. 14	123. 45	124. 60	125. 9	126. 32

127. 6   128. 14   129. 1   130. 4   131. 11   132. 7   133. 5

134. 4   135. 3   136. 5   137. 11   138. 9   139. 4   140. 8

141. 2   142. 7   143. 99   144. 3   145. 8   146. 6   147. 1

148. 2   149. 9   150. 50   151. 20   152. 3   153. 1   154. 12

155. 1   156. 5   157. 35   158. 12   159. 8   160. 9   161. 16

162. 7   163. 4   164. 7   165. 48   166. 5   167. 36   168. 10

169. 64   170. 10   171. 24   172. 18   173. 24   174. 24   175. 55

176. 35   177. 18   178. 60   179. 3   180. 6   181. 1   182. 63

183. 10   184. 5   185. 1   186. 5   187. 6   188. 3   189. 12

190. 16   191. 1   192. 4

Page 19: Percentage

193. 14   194. 800   195. 70   196. 80   197. 200

198. 8   199. 630   200. 2%   201. 80%   202. 4%

203. 8%   204. 600   205. 180   206. 72   207. 500

208. 500   209. 90   210. 70%   211. 320   212. 1%

213. 14   214. 900   215. 1800   216. 100   217. 180

218. 90%   219. 21   220. 40%   221. 54   222. 100

223. 15%   224. 5%   225. 200   226. 200   227. 30%

228. 35%   229. 40   230. 450   231. 3%   232. 100

233. 100%   234. 40%   235. 8%   236. 70   237. 1000

238. 20%   239. 500   240. 480   241. 270   242. 28

243. 525   244. 5%   245. 15%   246. 7%   247. 2

248. 900   249. 300   250. 80%   251. 35%   252. 900

253. 6%   254. 90   255. 4%   256. 30%   257. 40%

258. 150   259. 400   260. 400   261. 140   262. 400

263. 6   264. 3.2   265. 12   266. 400   267. 40

268. 100   269. 700   270. 300   271. 18   272. 42

273. 4   274. 75   275. 100   276. 100%   277. 7

278. 70   279. 5%   280. 315   281. 100   282. 20

283. 480   284. 800   285. 45   286. 60   287. 180

288. 100   289. 300   290. 105   291. 300   292. 48

Page 27: Percent

293. 275.643   294. 1.5%   295. 0.063   296. 0.294

297. 5.5%   298. 9.28   299. 2   300. 52

301. 14.322   302. 28.7%   303. 2   304. 2.496

305. 0.2%   306. 5.3%   307. 53.38   308. 17.2%

309. 0.7%   310. 553   311. 0.33   312. 0.7%

313. 0.408   314. 6.832   315. 0.6%   316. 49.4%

317. 9.4%   318. 1.225   319. 885   320. 762

321. 9.8%   322. 0.756   323. 0.6%   324. 47

325. 0.111   326. 36.9%   327. 1.5%   328. 0.224

329. 2   330. 7   331. 42   332. 32.0%

333. 408

334. 28.7%

335. 0.089

336. 2

337. 1

338. 5.3%

339. 6.8%

340. 17.2%

341. 0.112

342. 614

343. 5.5%

344. 0.7%

345. 850

346. 160

347. 0.054

348. 103.246

349. 9.4%

350. 0.18

351. 73

352. 0.7%

353. 20

354. 8.4%

355. 0.6%

356. 54.488

357. 1.605

358. 36.9%

Page 34: Convert Percent and Decimals

359. 0.38
360. 67%
361. 0.83
362. 92%
363. 0.75
364. 98%

365. 51%
366. 27%
367. 0.41
368. 0.74
369. 0.91
370. 8%

371. 0.89
372. 0.04
373. 0.44
374. 0.18
375. 0.09
376. 0.34

377. 0.07
378. 60%
379. 0.82
380. 93%
381. 2%
382. 19%

383. 24%
384. 66%
385. 94%
386. 33%
387. 84%
388. 0.69

389. 0.59
390. 88%
391. 70%
392. 0.43
393. 0.72
394. 0.8

395. 0.54
396. 0.61
397. 0.96
398. 0.97
399. 0.12
400. 25%

401. 1%
402. 99%
403. 57%
404. 0.79
405. 29%
406. 3%

407. 42%
408. 39%
409. 0.31
410. 0.56
411. 0.48
412. 21%

413. 100%
414. 0.65
415. 0.95
416. 0.81
417. 0.73
418. 0.87

Page 39: Word Problems: Percent

419. 8
420. $108.00
421. 6
422. $8.00

423. $3.00
424. $25.00
425. 28
426. $63.00

427. $21.00   428. 94   429. 23   430. $19.00

431. 14   432. 33   433. 2   434. 76

435. 18   436. $10.00   437. 2   438. $101.00

439. 18   440. 105   441. $21.00   442. 2

443. 26   444. 1   445. $25.00   446. 1

447. 84   448. 38   449. 12   450. 19

451. 50   452. $20.00   453. 16   454. $5.00

455. $5.00   456. $109.00   457. 34   458. $58.00

459. 6   460. $106.00   461. 1   462. $93.00

463. $76.00   464. 2   465. 6   466. 12

467. $52.00   468. $110.00

Page 50: Convert: Ratio, Fraction, Percent, and Decimals

469.

	Ratio	Fraction	Percent	Decimal
a.	17:18	17/18	94.4%	0.944
b.	1:1	1/1	100%	1
c.	2:11	2/11	18.2%	0.182
d.	4:12	4/12	33.3%	0.333
e.	2:19	2/19	10.5%	0.105
f.	1:7	1/7	14.3%	0.143
g.	9:10	9/10	90%	0.9
h.	1:2	1/2	50%	0.5
i.	3:7	3/7	42.9%	0.429
j.	12:15	12/15	80%	0.8
k.	5:17	5/17	29.4%	0.294
l.	1:4	1/4	25%	0.25
m.	11:14	11/14	78.6%	0.786
n.	3:20	3/20	15%	0.15
o.	4:14	4/14	28.6%	0.286

470.

	Ratio	Fraction	Percent	Decimal
a.	2:8	2/8	25%	0.25
b.	9:14	9/14	64.3%	0.643
c.	5:7	5/7	71.4%	0.714
d.	6:9	6/9	66.7%	0.667
e.	2:2	2/2	100%	1
f.	1:2	1/2	50%	0.5
g.	1:3	1/3	33.3%	0.333
h.	19:20	19/20	95%	0.95
i.	2:7	2/7	28.6%	0.286
j.	1:7	1/7	14.3%	0.143
k.	10:11	10/11	90.9%	0.909
l.	6:7	6/7	85.7%	0.857
m.	2:4	2/4	50%	0.5
n.	10:14	10/14	71.4%	0.714
o.	3:14	3/14	21.4%	0.214

471.

	Ratio	Fraction	Percent	Decimal
a.	8:8	8/8	100%	1
b.	6:12	6/12	50%	0.5
c.	10:14	10/14	71.4%	0.714
d.	2:7	2/7	28.6%	0.286
e.	11:15	11/15	73.3%	0.733
f.	1:5	1/5	20%	0.2
g.	1:2	1/2	50%	0.5
h.	11:13	11/13	84.6%	0.846
i.	3:4	3/4	75%	0.75
j.	3:19	3/19	15.8%	0.158
k.	10:17	10/17	58.8%	0.588
l.	7:11	7/11	63.6%	0.636
m.	2:3	2/3	66.7%	0.667
n.	2:6	2/6	33.3%	0.333
o.	5:7	5/7	71.4%	0.714

472.

	Ratio	Fraction	Percent	Decimal
a.	4:10	4/10	40%	0.4
b.	8:8	8/8	100%	1
c.	1:3	1/3	33.3%	0.333
d.	7:13	7/13	53.8%	0.538
e.	4:6	4/6	66.7%	0.667
f.	3:19	3/19	15.8%	0.158
g.	4:8	4/8	50%	0.5
h.	6:12	6/12	50%	0.5
i.	3:16	3/16	18.8%	0.188
j.	2:3	2/3	66.7%	0.667
k.	9:16	9/16	56.2%	0.562
l.	7:8	7/8	87.5%	0.875
m.	1:8	1/8	12.5%	0.125
n.	1:7	1/7	14.3%	0.143
o.	1:9	1/9	11.1%	0.111

473.

	Ratio	Fraction	Percent	Decimal
a.	1:17	1/17	5.9%	0.059
b.	5:5	5/5	100%	1
c.	3:14	3/14	21.4%	0.214
d.	3:4	3/4	75%	0.75
e.	4:10	4/10	40%	0.4
f.	4:5	4/5	80%	0.8
g.	1:4	1/4	25%	0.25
h.	14:20	14/20	70%	0.7
i.	3:18	3/18	16.7%	0.167
j.	6:10	6/10	60%	0.6
k.	11:12	11/12	91.7%	0.917
l.	4:11	4/11	36.4%	0.364
m.	12:18	12/18	66.7%	0.667
n.	3:6	3/6	50%	0.5
o.	9:15	9/15	60%	0.6

474.

	Ratio	Fraction	Percent	Decimal
a.	3:3	3/3	100%	1
b.	3:5	3/5	60%	0.6
c.	5:10	5/10	50%	0.5
d.	4:6	4/6	66.7%	0.667
e.	4:13	4/13	30.8%	0.308
f.	2:4	2/4	50%	0.5
g.	15:17	15/17	88.2%	0.882
h.	9:12	9/12	75%	0.75
i.	5:6	5/6	83.3%	0.833
j.	10:13	10/13	76.9%	0.769
k.	6:11	6/11	54.5%	0.545
l.	3:11	3/11	27.3%	0.273
m.	9:10	9/10	90%	0.9
n.	6:20	6/20	30%	0.3
o.	6:19	6/19	31.6%	0.316

475.

	Ratio	Fraction	Percent	Decimal
a.	1:1	1/1	100%	1
b.	11:12	11/12	91.7%	0.917
c.	9:15	9/15	60%	0.6
d.	7:12	7/12	58.3%	0.583
e.	2:3	2/3	66.7%	0.667
f.	7:16	7/16	43.8%	0.438
g.	8:19	8/19	42.1%	0.421
h.	3:4	3/4	75%	0.75
i.	6:7	6/7	85.7%	0.857
j.	13:14	13/14	92.9%	0.929
k.	3:7	3/7	42.9%	0.429
l.	2:15	2/15	13.3%	0.133
m.	4:5	4/5	80%	0.8
n.	18:19	18/19	94.7%	0.947
o.	2:5	2/5	40%	0.4

476.

	Ratio	Fraction	Percent	Decimal
a.	1:5	1/5	20%	0.2
b.	1:1	1/1	100%	1
c.	1:17	1/17	5.9%	0.059
d.	5:8	5/8	62.5%	0.625
e.	1:6	1/6	16.7%	0.167
f.	15:19	15/19	78.9%	0.789
g.	13:20	13/20	65%	0.65
h.	5:6	5/6	83.3%	0.833
i.	3:18	3/18	16.7%	0.167
j.	9:11	9/11	81.8%	0.818
k.	6:14	6/14	42.9%	0.429
l.	3:14	3/14	21.4%	0.214
m.	3:9	3/9	33.3%	0.333
n.	2:16	2/16	12.5%	0.125
o.	2:15	2/15	13.3%	0.133

477.

	Ratio	Fraction	Percent	Decimal
a.	13:16	13/16	81.2%	0.812
b.	14:20	14/20	70%	0.7
c.	8:11	8/11	72.7%	0.727
d.	1:1	1/1	100%	1
e.	2:3	2/3	66.7%	0.667
f.	1:20	1/20	5%	0.05
g.	2:14	2/14	14.3%	0.143
h.	1:2	1/2	50%	0.5
i.	8:17	8/17	47.1%	0.471
j.	15:17	15/17	88.2%	0.882
k.	8:18	8/18	44.4%	0.444
l.	2:7	2/7	28.6%	0.286
m.	1:4	1/4	25%	0.25
n.	2:15	2/15	13.3%	0.133
o.	12:18	12/18	66.7%	0.667

478.

	Ratio	Fraction	Percent	Decimal
a.	3:5	3/5	60%	0.6
b.	4:17	4/17	23.5%	0.235
c.	11:13	11/13	84.6%	0.846
d.	2:16	2/16	12.5%	0.125
e.	7:9	7/9	77.8%	0.778
f.	1:6	1/6	16.7%	0.167
g.	8:11	8/11	72.7%	0.727
h.	1:1	1/1	100%	1
i.	11:19	11/19	57.9%	0.579
j.	3:7	3/7	42.9%	0.429
k.	18:19	18/19	94.7%	0.947
l.	1:5	1/5	20%	0.2
m.	6:16	6/16	37.5%	0.375
n.	5:6	5/6	83.3%	0.833
o.	1:9	1/9	11.1%	0.111